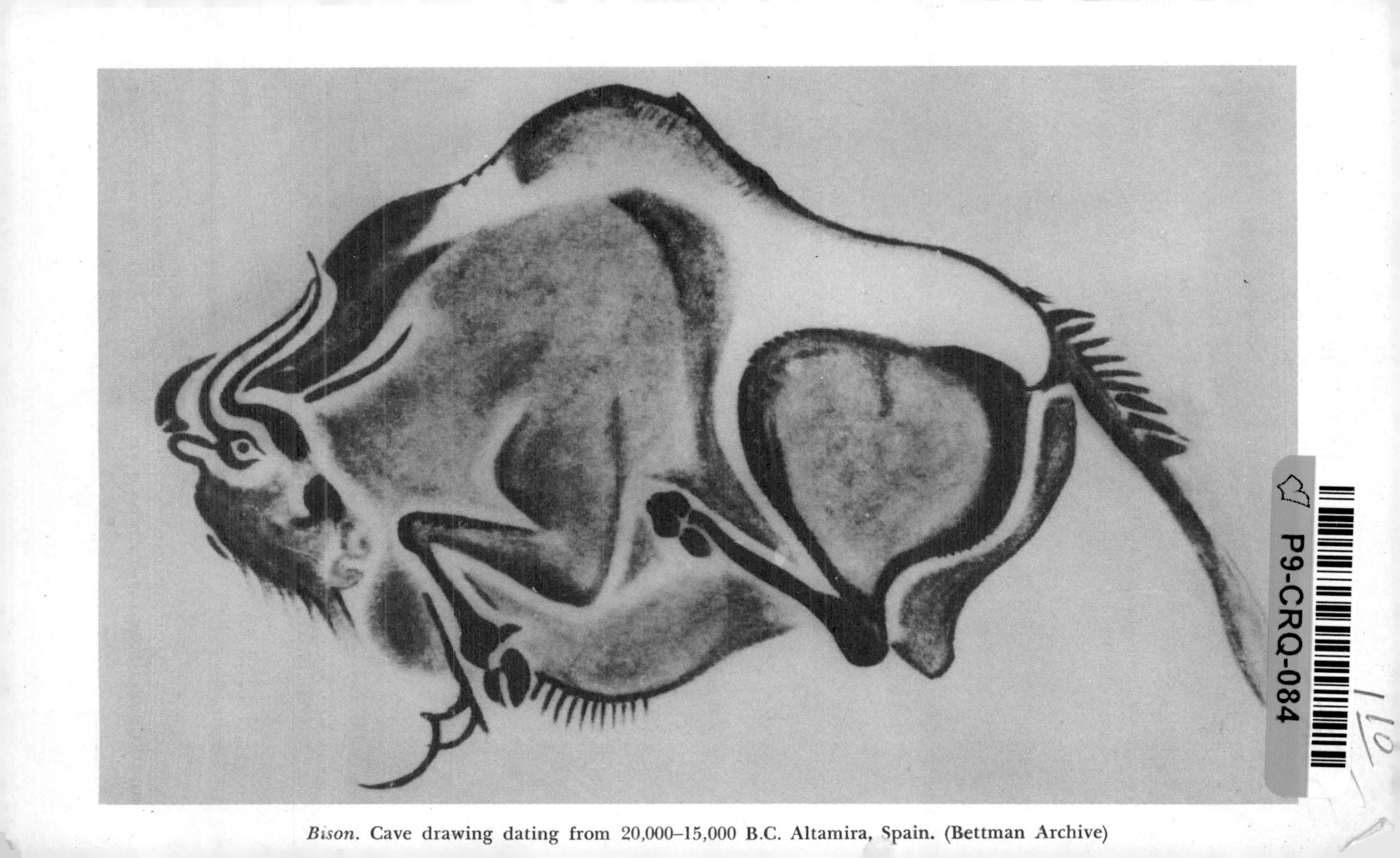

Bison. Cave drawing dating from 20,000–15,000 B.C. Altamira, Spain. (Bettman Archive)

ABOUT THE AUTHOR

Casper de Jong, who teaches art at The Hague, has written many articles on art and has translated several works in the field (among others, *Vincent van Gogh* by Julius Meier-Graefe). In his lectures and courses he has dedicated himself with great enthusiasm to the history of art and the aesthetic appreciation of paintings. The conception of *Schilderijen zien* (*Paintings of the Western World*) follows naturally from his interests and activities.

ABOUT THE TRANSLATOR

Hans Koningsberger, who was born in Amsterdam, Holland, studied at the University of Zurich and has traveled widely in Europe and the Far East; he now lives in New York. A writer by profession, he has been highly acclaimed for his three novels: *The Affair, An American Romance,* and *A Walk with Love and Death.* Several articles by Mr. Koningsberger have appeared in *The New Yorker,* and he has also written *An Introduction to Modern Dutch Painting.* He has translated several works from the Dutch and French languages into English, among which are novels by Maria Dermoût and a selection of modern Dutch poetry.

John Sedgwick, who wrote the concluding chapter, "The Role of American Painting," especially for this edition, received his A.B. at Williams College and his M.A. and Ph.D. degrees at Harvard University. He has taught art history at Columbia University and Hunter College and is presently Professor of Art at the University of North Carolina at Greensboro. Professor Sedgwick is the author of *Art Appreciation* and *Structure and Evolution of the Major Cultures,* and co-author (with E. M. Upjohn) of *An Illustrated History of Art.*

EVERYDAY HANDBOOKS

PAINTINGS of the WESTERN WORLD

BY CASPER DE JONG

(Translated from the Dutch by Hans Koningsberger)

With a concluding chapter written by John Sedgwick
University of North Carolina at Greensboro

BARNES & NOBLE, INC.

PUBLISHERS · BOOKSELLERS · SINCE 1873

Second Printing, 1964

L. C. Catalogue Card Number: 63–19460

Original Dutch edition:
Schilderijen zien © 1958 by Het Spectrum, Utrecht

PRINTED IN THE UNITED STATES OF AMERICA

TABLE OF CONTENTS

LIST OF ILLUSTRATIONS

PART I

1

Looking at Paintings

When the American painter Whistler brought suit for libel against the art critic Ruskin, he was asked at the trial: "Would you explain to the gentlemen of the jury what art is?" Whistler looked at his interrogator and answered simply, "No." We should not pretend to know more about art than Whistler. The essence, the "this is it" quality of a work of art, rising out of the emotion and the creative imagination of its maker, remains a mystery.

"People who try to explain paintings are usually on the wrong track," Picasso has been quoted as saying. Generally, artists are suspicious of any explication of works of art, because, in the last analysis, the mental and spiritual process behind the creation of art cannot be defined. The beauty of a work of art has to be felt. One needs the ability to penetrate and share the vision of the artist; lacking such ability, one may develop it. An artist does not see people and things in an everyday sort of way. Anyone who observes everything soberly and without emotion, who cannot look at the world with amazement and awe, will never reach a true enjoyment of art. It is necessary above all to be receptive.

Is it impossible, then, to learn how to look at and appreciate paintings? Certainly not. No art critic, connoisseur, or collector would dare say he was born with a developed sensitivity. Often people just beginning to be interested in art think of some works as beautiful which they later realize are completely superficial. But why should one feel ashamed of that? It is only unfortunate if one does not develop deeper insights during a lifetime.

Many people feel somewhat at a loss in a museum. They see numerous paintings, and they may know that there is much more to be appreciated than what immediately attracts them. Or, once they have seen the most famous painting in a museum, they may assume that the others do not matter. There was a cartoon in the *New Yorker* magazine of a couple dashing into the Louvre and asking the guard: "Where's the 'Mona Lisa'? Quick, we're double-parked." Yet, the Louvre has paintings whose artistic value is as high as that of the "Mona Lisa." Sometimes a simple painting by a little-known artist is more moving than an elaborate Renaissance or seventeenth-century pageant.

The best way to gain better understanding and greater enjoyment of art is to view many paintings. By going to museums and exhibitions and looking at the paintings thoughtfully and earnestly one will gain an initial familiarity with the various artists and styles. From this initial rapport with the works one may move on to an increasingly satisfying appreciation. And since good intentions alone are not enough, here are a few helpful suggestions:

1. Take the trouble to learn about the materials and techniques used in painting but do not identify art with technical perfection.
2. Learn something about the artistic background of a painter's works, especially the styles and values of his period, before judging his creations.
3. Acquire some idea of the development of painting from the Middle Ages to modern times. Each period looks for its own means of expression; each is a continuation of, and a reaction against, what has preceded it.
4. Try to look at each painting anew and to understand what the artist has attempted to communicate.
5. Be aware that a painting is not a photographic representation of nature and do not think that the subject determines the value of a painting.
6. Avoid the kind of snobbishness which believes only in works created in one particular time or place, or by one artist.

With these suggestions in mind it is possible to look at paintings as a whole and to obtain a total impression. Some paintings are meant to be viewed from a distance only—for example, those of the Impressionists. (But there is a story about Rembrandt, which relates that when people came up too close to his paintings the master would draw them back with the comment, "The smell of the paint would bother you.") Other paintings, especially those of the Flemish period, should be examined close-up because of the care which the artist lavished upon the smallest details.

After viewing the painting as a whole, one should look at its parts, letting the gaze wander over it; one should try to discover the methods used in its composition, to observe its rhythm, its harmony, the contrast between its colors (particularly the alternation of light and dark parts), and the way the paint has been applied.

In most cases the subject will not present many problems. If it does—as for instance in paintings of biblical or historical subjects, legends of saints, or allegorical figures—the catalogue will usually give some information. In those works which have a mysterious subject, such as "The Tempest" by Giorgione or "The Garden of Delights" by Hieronymus Bosch, there is nothing wrong in letting the mystery remain one. The stimulation of the imagination is often more important than an intellectual explanation.

By comparing paintings, one becomes aware of the different ways in which a painter can express himself. Only then will judgment grow keener and power of criticism more certain, and this judgment, based upon developed insight and understanding, is as valid as any.

2

The Painting as a Work of Art

A painting combines colors, lines, and forms in such a way as to express an emotion, an idea, or a mood. It manifests a personal vision, consciously or unconsciously arrived at, a feeling for color and form, and a personal way of treating the subject.

Maurice Denis, one of the first Symbolist painters, has defined a painting as "a plane covered with colors in a certain pattern." Such a plane is, as a rule, rectangular, although in a few cases it is round, oval, or diamond-shaped. A painting has definite shape and a frame which separates it from its surroundings. Whatever its physical aspects, it reveals a new world—one which may or may not resemble visual reality, but which never simply copies it. As a mere copy, it could not be called art, for art is expression, not a reproduction. What the *painter sees* is only the starting point, the motif which moves him. What the *painting expresses* makes it a work of art. "The painter paints to free himself of his feelings and his vision," said Picasso. The spectator, however, has to discover what the painter wants to express and to what degree he has succeeded.

A museum visitor might say: "When I look at Rembrandt's masterpiece 'Saul and David,' I see how the painter was moved by the old story and how majestically he has revealed the inner life of a man. His painting touches me. But how can I be moved by a painting that shows a part of a table and on it a plate, a knife, a glass, and a lemon?" Well, perhaps the harmony of the colors or the play of the light gives unexpected life to the object. We should not forget that Rembrandt also etched a little shell with painstaking care, and that Dürer created scenes of the Apocalypse, a blade of grass, and a squirrel—each with equal attention. The miracle of creation can be depicted through the greatest or the least of its own phenomena.

When we turn to the personal element in painting, we find great variation among individual artists. Vermeer, Cézanne, Seurat, and Mondrian were very conscious of what they were striving for. Chagall and Van Gogh seem to have created their works more spontaneously. Van Gogh once wrote: "At certain times I am no longer conscious of what I do, and the painting comes into existence as in a dream."

The source of the artist's creative experience may likewise vary. Rembrandt, Bosch, and El Greco were motivated by what they felt in their hearts and souls, whereas the seventeenth-century Dutch master Frans Hals and the nineteenth-century Impressionists were inspired by what their eyes saw. A differentiation can thus be made between painting based on inner perception and that based on sensory perception.

Yet, many a painting did not come into existence solely because of an initial creative urge of the artist. There was another, quite simple reason: the commission. It should not be assumed, however, that the fact of the commission diminishes the artistic value. On the contrary, many great works were painted on commission. Leonardo da Vinci's "Mona Lisa," Raphael's "Sistine Madonna," Michelangelo's frescoes in the Sistine Chapel, and Rembrandt's "The Night Watch" were all commissioned by patrons. And Picasso's "Guernica," to cite a recent example, was painted on order for the Spanish pavilion in the Paris World's Fair of 1937. In each instance, of course, the artists interpreted the patrons' directions in their own way.

In their search for expression, however, painters have often met opposition from public opinion. When the Paris Impressionists had their first exhibition in 1874, the public was astonished by the way these painters viewed the world; a few decades later, however, everyone could *see* their way, but could not understand the paintings of the Expressionists and the Cubists.

Great artists arrive at their own modes of expression; the less gifted ones follow in their footsteps. John Constable was aware of this when in 1829 he wrote in his preface to the *English Landscape:*

> In art, there are two modes by which men aim at distinction. In the one, by a careful application to what others have accomplished, the artist imitates their works, or selects and combines their various beauties; in the other, he seeks excellence at its primitive source, nature. . . . The results of the one mode, as they repeat that with which the eye is already familiar, are soon recognized and estimated, while the advances of the artist in a new path must necessarily be slow, for few are able to judge of that which deviates from the usual course, or are qualified to appreciate original studies.

What Constable discussed at some length, Gauguin expressed in a few words: "In art you are either a revolutionary or a plagiarist." Perhaps these words are too harsh, for only the very great artist can create a revolution. Most artists, however, begin by imitating an admired master but in time develop their own style, and it would be unjust to call them plagiarists.

Why is it that a painting depicting a beautiful woman or a sweet child may not be significant as art at all, whereas a hideously distorted woman's face by Picasso receives acclaim as great art? The answer is clear: The inept painter has been preoccupied with sentiments which have nothing to do with art, while Picasso's work, on the other hand, gives the viewer a fresh vision of mankind. That vision may or may not be accepted in its bitterness and irony, but it cannot be denied that such an example is genuine art.

Thus, it is clear that the significant personal element in a painting is what distinguishes the artist from the craftsman. This personal touch is found in each element of a painting—in its subject, in its design and colors, and in its style.

It would be well to consider for a moment the artist's concern with his subject in the world of visible phenomena, nature. We have called the world of the painting imaginary, and this statement poses the important question: *What is the relationship between art and nature?*

When prehistoric man painted animals on the walls of caves, his art bordered on magic. These pictures served as substitutes for real animals, and the magician of the tribe, sometimes shown too, performed a ritual dance. In some instances the hunters shot arrows at the picture animals. All this was part of the magic rite which, it was believed, would help the hunter catch the real game. Murals in Egyptian tombs had a similar magical meaning. In these dark enclosed places their only purpose was to serve the dead as substitutes for reality. Even now a picture of a man or an animal is almost identical with the real thing in the minds of some primitive peoples.

Ancient Greece admired above all the ability of the painter to make things seem almost real. "Art imitates nature," Aristotle said. And Greek writers have told many anecdotes about this artistic imitation. There is the story of a cow sculptured by Myron which looked so real that a cowherd swung his stick at it. A tale about a painting by Zeuxis, showing a boy holding some grapes, also comes to mind. When sparrows flew down to pick at the grapes, the friends of the master congratulated him on his success; but Zeuxis shook his head and complained, "If only I had painted the boy better the birds would have been afraid of him."

Antiquity was followed by a period of more than a thousand years during which art abandoned realistic reproduction and turned toward the representation of the transcendental. Medieval art may be called symbolic; it used the forms of earthly reality to express another, a divine reality. But, when the Renaissance awakened interest in earthliness, naturalism was again revived. The illusion of the "almost real" is still an important part of our enjoyment of paintings; often a museum guard may point to some favorite work and ask us to admire the true-to-life details. In the nineteenth century this idea of art as imitation of nature reached its climax. If a painting looked exactly like its subject, the public considered it the highest form of art. The poet Baudelaire, who was also a highly perceptive art critic, wrote in 1859: "The upper classes believe in Nature and only in Nature. They think that art cannot be anything but reproduction of Nature."

This was also the time when "panoramas" became fashionable. When the visitor looked at them, he had the impression that he was standing in a real landscape. These panoramas may be well painted, but it is doubtful that they can be called great art.

Art begins where imitation of nature ends. Delacroix wrote in his diary that a "painting must be more than a picture to a man with imagination. The meaning of a painting is found in what cannot be defined or described. It is that which is added to the lines and colors by the soul in order to speak to another soul." Elsewhere in his diary he noted: "Nature is only a dictionary. We go to her to find the right tone, the particular form, just as we look up the spelling of a word in a dictionary. But a dictionary is not considered a literary masterpiece and neither is nature a model. The painter goes to find suggestions for basic values, but the harmony which he instills is the work *of his imagination alone*." Still another passage in his correspondence reads: "A man has innate feelings which will never be satisfied by real things. The imagination of the painter gives form and life to these feelings."

Toward the end of the nineteenth century—with Van Gogh, Gauguin, Cézanne, and others—the movement away from nature gained full force and even extends into the present day. It is no coincidence that in this same period photography took over from art the task of restoring reality.

But the question arises: What about the work of those painters we call "realists," those who adhere strictly to visible reality—painters like Vermeer and Courbet? Are they not artists? Of course they are, and quite superior ones. They saw nature with such penetrating concentration and intensity that they brought her to life for us. In their works visual reality achieves a clarity which becomes a revelation. But these painters, precise though they were, did not create photographic copies. They were engaged in a personal re-creation of reality and showed us everyday things in an uncommon way. At the other end of the scale a nonrealistic painter like Chagall might consider himself a realist, for he shows us exactly what he sees in his own mind.

In the relation between art and natural reality we find three stages with many intermediate forms:

1. The painter portrays nature; this is what we usually call *realism*. Examples are seventeenth-century Dutch art and most of the art of the nineteenth century.
2. The painter changes nature; he ennobles it, like Raphael, or distorts it like El Greco, Van Gogh, and Picasso.
3. The painter completely abandons nature. This is the Nonobjective art of our century, with Kandinsky and Mondrian as examples.

Between the two extremes—realism and nonrepresentation—there unfolds, to use the words of René Huyghe, the French art scholar, "an infinite number of variations, in which we find the various nuances that have distinguished art throughout its history."

3

The Subject

Looking at paintings introduces the spectator to a great variety of subject matter. Some subjects he may appreciate, some he may not. One person likes still-life paintings, another prefers portraits. One admires a pair of old worn-out shoes painted by Van Gogh; another enjoys a work by Rembrandt showing a slaughtered ox in a butcher's shop. A landscape is most easily appreciated by those who love the countryside—but for reasons which have nothing to do with art.

A work of art has to be judged as such and not by its subject alone. It isn't the *what* but the *how* that matters. Matisse has written: "When I see a painting, I forget its subject; important are only lines, forms and colors." And this attitude is shared by the numerous twentieth-century artists who have painted in the abstract because they want the painting to be judged as a work of art and not as mere illustration. In his own work, however, Matisse did not completely ignore his subject. Some of his paintings are variations on a single motif: a young woman and flowers in an interior setting. Thus, he must have needed such a subject as a means of expression. It would be correct to say that the subject of a painting, though not in itself important, becomes important as art through the way in which it is presented by the painter in terms of line, form, and color.

Nevertheless, we must realize that throughout long periods of art history the subject was of paramount importance. In fact, the farther back in history we go, the more difficult it becomes to detach a work of art from its subject. To begin with, in prehistoric art the realistic portrayal of wild animals had a functional significance. The subject was also of primary importance during the Middle Ages, when the artist had to represent his religious subjects in prescribed detail. Not until the Renaissance did artists enjoy greater freedom to choose and interpret their own subjects.

The gradual emancipation of the painter, whereby he achieved freedom to select his subject matter, occurred in the fifteenth and sixteenth centuries, with the transition from religious to worldly subjects. Until the time of Jan van Eyck saints and altarpieces were shown against a gold background. With Van Eyck, Rogier van der Weyden, Hugo van der Goes, and, especially, Dirk Bouts, the gold background gave way to a landscape. In 1507 Gerard David's "Baptism of Christ in the Jordan" had a landscape for its setting, and Joachim Patinir portrayed Mary and Joseph on the flight to Egypt as tiny figures in a wide countryside. Jan Mostaert and Albrecht Altdorfer also created landscapes in which there are no saintly figures.

In addition to the landscape, other subjects on fifteenth-century altarpieces—the donors, for instance—indicate how secular interests were introduced into the sacred subject. In the beginning it was customary for the pious donors to have themselves depicted as spectators viewing the holy scene. The donors were modestly painted in the background or at one side and were much smaller than the main figures. Later, they were larger and appeared in the foreground, along with their wives and children. Occasionally, the donors appeared in the roles of the sacred figures. In the "Nativity" by Rogier van der Weyden, Peter Bladelin (the donor) kneels opposite Joseph before the Virgin and Child; in the works of Botticelli and Gozzoli, the Three Kings are members of the Medici family. And the frescoes of Ghirlandajo in the choir of the church of Santa Maria Novella in Florence, which are supposed to show the lives of Mary and John the Baptist, are really a kind of family album of the banker Giovanni Tornabuoni.

Since there are innumerable topics which may serve as subjects for paintings, let us classify them, for purposes of discussion, as follows:

The Christian Religion. For more than one thousand years —from the second century until the beginning of the Renaissance late in the fourteenth century—painting drew on Christianity for much of its subject matter. Even after the Renaissance, deep religious feeling remained a source of inspiration for the great masters: in Italy, for Raphael, Michelangelo, Titian, and Tintoretto; in Spain, for El Greco and Murillo; in Flanders, for Rubens and his school; and in Holland, for Rembrandt, who painted biblical scenes of great dramatic force, although no church commissioned him to do so. After the eighteenth century, however, important religious paintings became sporadic. In the nineteenth century Delacroix and Maurice Denis were prominent in this field. In the twentieth century Georges Rouault remains one of the few interpreters of Christian themes.

Mythology and History. During the periods of great art—the Renaissance, the Baroque, the Rococo, and Neoclassicism—mythological subjects were very popular and were used by famous painters from Botticelli and Titian to Rubens, Poussin, and Ingres. During the first half of the nineteenth century, the period of Romanticism, historical subjects were very much in vogue. Most of these works, often of enormous size, have little artistic value because they concentrate too much on the subject, on the careful delineation of all the facts, the setting, the costumes, and other details.

What moves us in an important historical painting is the artist's vision of character and tragic conflict. Historical accuracy, so highly prized in the nineteenth century, interferes with the appreciation of a work of art if it distracts attention from the artist's interpretation. In the seventeenth century famous paintings depicting historical subjects include works by Rembrandt and Velázquez. In the Romantic period important historical works were created by Goya, David, and Delacroix.

The Portrait. The art of portrait painting begins to suggest how various are the meanings of the word "realism." Gothic art sought to picture man in the context of his faith, as a child of God. Titian, Rubens, Van Dyck, Velázquez, and Gainsborough emphasized the class and rank of their models. Holbein and Hals tried to portray the outward appearance of the individual with faithful objectivity. Rembrandt and, later, the Expressionists did not want to depict the outer man so much as his inner being. Rembrandt brought out the good in man; Picasso, the demoniacal. And the Impressionists painted man as he presented himself to their eyes for one fleeting moment.

At this point we should mention the first painted portraits of which we have any record. A fresco by Simone Martini, painted in the year 1328 on one of the walls of the Palazzo Pubblico in Siena, Italy, is considered the first independent portrait. It shows a heraldic figure against a landscape in which a castle and palisades are silhouetted against a night-blue sky. Actually more of a symbol than an individual portrait, it is the evidence of the pride of the citizens of the Town Republic in a victory over their great rival Florence. The first framed portrait, that of the French king Jean Le Bon, was probably produced by Gérard d'Orleans in the year 1360. Although painted on a gold background, it is much more individual in its conception than the Martini painting. In 1431 Jan van Eyck painted the first personal portraits—those of the donors Jodocus Vydt and Isabella Borluut on the two side wings of the altarpiece at Ghent. Van Eyck was also the first to paint a double portrait: the famous painting (from 1434) of the Italian merchant, "Giovanni Arnolfini and his Wife," which is also, incidentally, the earliest portrait in an interior setting.

In the northern Netherlands we find a special kind of portrait —the group portrait of colleges, regents of orphanages, groups of guards. Famous examples of these portraits in Dutch art are Rembrandt's "The Anatomy Lesson of Dr. Tulp," "The Night Watch," and "Syndics of the Cloth Guild" and Frans Hals's "Regents of the St. Elizabeth Hospital." These portraits fulfilled two purposes: the presentation of a good likeness of each individual and the expression of the spirit and typical activity of the group. Thus, colleges of governors are usually shown deliberating in a meeting. The problem of the "guard" paintings was more difficult; it was solved by either showing the guards preparing to march (as in Rembrandt's "Night Watch") or portraying them at a festive dinner (as in Frans Hals's "Banquet of the Civic Guard of Archers of St. George in Haarlem").

In a separate category is the self-portrait in which the artist strikes an attitude or at times shows himself with searching realism. Rembrandt's self-portraits, masterpieces of self-scrutiny, are an outstanding record of the artist's soul.

The Landscape. Although the first natural and realistic landscape, a view of the Danube Valley near Regensburg, was painted about 1530 by Albrecht Altdorfer, paintings with recognizable topographic features had appeared much earlier: French castles and towns, in the miniatures of the brothers Limbourg around the beginning of the fifteenth century, and a view from the shores of Lake Geneva, on an altarpiece by Konrad Witz, in 1444. These were intended not as independent landscapes but as background for human activity. Two small panels by Gerard David, which are now in The Hague, are the earliest known forest views. The first real seascape—a very romantic painting, complete with storm, high waves, and an open-mouthed whale pursuing a ship—was painted by Pieter Bruegel about 1560.

In landscape paintings the work of different artists may reveal very different visions. Pieter Bruegel, one of the first great landscape painters, used the landscape as the stage for human activity in various seasons. In seventeenth-century Holland landscape painting flourished, and many painters became specialists in the technique. They created "realistic" landscapes—varying in mood from the sunny, cheerful ones of Cuyp and Hobbema to the melancholy ones of Jacob von Ruisdael and the impressionistic works of Jan van Goyen. Perhaps the most impressive landscapes have been painted by artists who were not specialists in this field: Rubens and Rembrandt. Consider for a moment Rubens' "Château de Steen" and Rembrandt's "Stormy Landscape."

The nineteenth century replaced the seventeenth as the next period of great landscape art. Beginning in England with Constable and Turner, the predecessors of Impressionism, and in Germany with the romantic works of Caspar David Friedrich, it flowered in France with the Barbizon painters and in Holland with the School of The Hague. The French Impressionists further developed the landscape, as did Van Gogh and Cézanne. In the twentieth century some of the Expressionist painters who have painted successfully in this field are the Norwegian Munch and the Austrian Kokoschka.

The Architectural Painting. Architectural painting, a category which includes towns, separate buildings, and interiors and exteriors, had its origins in the altarpiece. The earliest example was probably the one created by Geertgen for the St. Bavon

Church in Haarlem, painted sometime prior to 1490. Jan van Eyck and Rogier van der Weyden also painted sacred subjects in Gothic church settings. In the seventeenth century architectural painting became separate and distinct from other types and received great impetus from the paintings of churches (by Saenredam) and of towns (by Jan van der Heyden). Here again, many famous town views were painted by nonspecialists—El Greco ("View of Toledo") and Vermeer ("View of Delft"). In the twentieth century, views of Paris, especially of Montmartre, found a gifted and colorful interpreter in Maurice Utrillo.

The Genre Painting. The genre painting portrays scenes from ordinary life—human beings in their everyday indoor and outdoor activities. Pieter Bruegel's peasant scenes were among the first in this category, which again reached its artistic summit in seventeenth-century Holland with Vermeer, Adriaen van Ostade, Jan Steen, and Pieter de Hooch. Eighteenth-century France excelled in this area with Chardin her greatest master. In the nineteenth century, Romanticism revived the genre painting—this time with anecdotic overtones.

The Still Life. The still life, more than the genre piece, can be said to represent the pure art of painting because it is concerned mainly with problems of color and form. In addition, a still life can have symbolic meaning through the choice of its subject: flowers and fruit express the joys of life, while the objects of the so-called *vanitas* still lifes—a skull, an hourglass, or a broken vase—suggest the brevity of human existence. Van Gogh is an excellent example of an artist who used symbolism in his still lifes; his sunflowers, for instance, represent the sun itself. Another Van Gogh still life—showing a pipe, a book on medicine, a letter, and other objects—was painted in Arles soon after the artist experienced great emotional stress and reflects his intense determination to surmount that crisis.

In seventeenth-century Netherlands there were many still-life painters whose special subjects were the hunt, breakfast scenes, and groupings of rich crystal and china. Famous French painters of still lifes were Courbet, Manet, and Cézanne. The Cubists Picasso and Braque, who painted the still life in their search for constructive patterns of the picture plane, employed a limited choice of subjects: musical instruments, glasses, fruit bowls.

The first independent still life, an anonymous work painted around 1475, shows a little cupboard, bottles, and a book. A few years later, in 1504, Jacopo de Barbari, who worked in Nuremberg and Brussels, painted what was for a long time accepted as the first still life—a dead partridge and some armor hung on a light-colored wall. Two other works, though not strictly independent ones because they were painted on the backs of other works, deserve mention: a Flemish painting by an unknown artist, depicting books and a basin (on the reverse side of a Madonna with Child dating from the year 1480); and a vase of lilies on the reverse of a man's portrait by Memling, painted shortly before 1494.

The Nude. Before the nineteenth century, the nude was not really a subject in its own right. Until then, nude figures had appeared only in biblical, mythological, and allegorical paintings—such as "Adam and Eve," "The Last Judgment," "Sleeping Venus," and "The Judgment of Paris." Again, Jan van Eyck was the first to paint realistic nudes—the Adam and Eve on his "Ghent Altarpiece." While the landscape, genre, and still life flourished in the North, Italy was greatly preoccupied with portraying the nude. It was under the influence of the Italian Renaissance that the nude appeared during the sixteenth century in French, Dutch, and German art. In the great compositions of Rubens and his school, the nude played a central role—but always in connection with mythological or allegorical subjects. Rubens made one exception: he painted an intimate likeness, the so-called Pelsken, of his young wife Hélène Fourment, and his will provided that the painting should remain her property after his death. Rembrandt, too, used his wife and close friends as nude models. Among his major works are his paintings of Saskia and Hendrickje Stoffels as Suzanna, Danaë, and Bathsheba. Nevertheless, it should be noted that, with the exception of these works by Rembrandt, the nude played no part in Dutch art until the nineteenth century. In Spanish art, too, the nude was a rarity; two famous works, however, are "Venus with a Mirror" by Velázquez and the "Maja Desnuda" by Goya. Nineteenth-century realism did not need a mythological or biblical pretext for painting a nude woman. If a painter wanted a setting, he used a natural one—the bath. Degas painted women bathing indoors; Courbet pictured them outdoors; and Renoir and the Swedish painter Zorn depicted them impressionistically in strong sunlight.

Nonobjective Painting. It is with some hesitation that we include Nonobjective painting in our list of subjects. The first such work was a water color painted by the Russian Kandinsky in 1910. Nonobjective works are alike in that they all lack any recognizable object, and we might call this art form a special genre.

It is difficult to classify paintings logically into distinct groups; any attempt to do so is necessarily artificial and imperfect. If we set up separate categories, such as portrait and landscape painting, we shall find some examples which do not fit precisely into one or the other: in some of Gainsborough's portraits, the landscapes are dominant features, and many eighteenth-century paintings of family scenes are really genre works of portraiture. Some paintings by Manet exemplify the same problem: Is his painting of Monet in the "Painting Barge" a landscape or a portrait? As for the abstractions of the twentieth century, it is necessary to forget completely the old categories.

4

The Painter's Materials and Techniques

For centuries the wall served as the foundation for paintings. The earliest paintings, produced fifteen to twenty thousand years ago in paleolithic times, are those on the walls and ceilings of caves in northern Spain (Altamira) and in southern France (Dordogne). One of the most recent discoveries was made in 1940 in a hillside near Montignac: the cave of Lascaux. The paintings on its walls, depicting bison, reindeer, and wild horses, are in good condition and still show evidence of the magical significance that was once given them.

The prehistoric artist achieved astonishing effects with his primitive means, and what strikes us most in these paintings is the amazing certainty of execution. Following the contours of the rock, he made his animals stand out in relief. In Lascaux only three colors were employed: brown-red, ocher-yellow, and black—a limited palette provided by charcoal, brownstone, and red and yellow iron oxide. The colors were mixed with fat and applied with the fingers or with a tampon of animal skin. In addition, a modern procedure of application was probably used: paint was often sprayed on the wall with a blowpipe.

The Egyptians painted the walls of their tombs at least 4,500 years ago. The oldest pictures are in relief, but in time, as many more colors became available, the artist began to use a smooth wall. The early conventions for the use of color—such as those prescribing the skin colors for figures, red-brown for men and yellow for women—were maintained while a wider range and freer use of color was developed, especially in such details as birds and fruits. Images from the life of the dead, painted in soft colors, give the tombs an almost festive appearance.

The Greeks, too, had a monumental school of wall painting. Nothing remains of it, but we can get an impression of what it was like from the Etruscan tombs in Italy and the villas of Pompeii, buried by Vesuvius in A.D. 79 and excavated in the eighteenth century. In the Villa dei Misteri, a house just outside the town gate of Pompeii, there is a room of beautiful murals preserved from ancient times; most of the other paintings have been removed to the Museum of Naples.

In the early Christian and Byzantine periods the churches of Rome, Ravenna, Torcello, and Venice were decorated with mosaics—decorations inlaid with small pieces of colored glass, enamel, or marble called *tesserae.* In the thirteenth century, however, mosaics were no longer in fashion, and artists began to do wall paintings using water colors on wet plaster. This method, called *fresco,* had to be executed very quickly since the plaster stayed wet only a day. The water in the wall mixed with the carbon dioxide in the air to give the paint a protective layer. The fresco painter had the wall plastered piece by piece and then, as soon as the plaster was on, painted it according to a prepared plan. He paid little attention to details and retouching was almost impossible. One of the greatest masters of the fresco technique was the fourteenth-century Florentine painter Giotto, whose murals in the San Francesco Church in Assisi and in the Arena Chapel in Padua began a new era in painting.

Most Italian Renaissance painters of the fifteenth century, starting with Masaccio, did frescoes and these are often their most important work. The art of fresco painting reached its peak in the sixteenth century with the decorations in the Vatican of the Sistine Chapel by Michelangelo and of the Stanza della Segnatura by Raphael. Fresco painting achieved its last triumph in the continuous tradition which began in the thirteenth century and ended with the magnificent art of the Venetian, Tiepolo, in the eighteenth century. Interest in the technique was not so high in the nineteenth century; thus, the murals by Puvis de Chavannes in the Pantheon in Paris and the water lilies of Claude Monet in the Orangerie in the Tuileries are in fact not frescoes but oil paintings on linen glued to the walls. A revival of true fresco technique has occured in our own century—with such Mexican artists as Siqueiros, Orozco, and Rivera.

Around 1300, when Giotto was painting his frescoes, the need arose for panel paintings that could be displayed in a sumptuous frame over an altar or in a side chapel to bring the narratives of the Bible and the Christian legends closer to the people. Until the end of the sixteenth century such paintings were generally done on wood panels—each a single piece of wood planed smooth or, for a larger work, several carefully joined planks. Because of warping over the centuries, however, these paintings often clearly show the cracks between the planks. In Italy the wood most often used was poplar; in Germany, pine or linden; and in the Netherlands, oak. Other woods were, of course, employed. Rembrandt, for instance, sometimes painted on costly mahogany. The kind of wood used can, therefore, furnish the art historian a clue to the country where an unidentified work of art originated.

The foundation of paintings was not, however, restricted to wood. Jan Bruegel and David Teniers painted on copper, and these works give a rather cold, metallic impression. Since the beginning of the seventeenth century, canvas stretched over a wooden framework has been used, although today many paintings are executed on cardboard, burlap, and other foundations.

Before the fifteenth century, panel paintings were executed in tempera, a kind of paint which was prepared with fresh egg yolks as the vehicle for the pigment and which (like the water colors used in frescoes) was quick-drying. Then, at the beginning of the fifteenth century, a radical innovation in painting was introduced when the brothers Van Eyck in Bruges "invented," according to legend, the oil technique. Actually this famous pair perfected a procedure of working with oils that had often been experimented with in the past. The advantage of oil painting lay chiefly in that the surface dried more slowly, making possible a more painstaking manner of working. This was compatible with the northern temperament and the Flemish tendency to create detailed, realistic representations—in contrast with the more monumental works of the Italians. In addition, the new technique answered the needs of Northern painters at a time when the Gothic view of the world, although still dominant, was finding expression in more and more realistic terms. After the time of the brothers Van Eyck, oils came into general use, and their influence gradually spread southward. Antonella da Messina was, in the fifteenth century, apparently the first Italian artist to use the technique.

Leonardo da Vinci experimented with oils in 1495 when he painted a mural, "The Last Supper," in the refectory of the Santa Maria delle Grazie in Milan. Unfortunately the results were poor: the paint began to flake off twenty years later, and all that is left today is a ruin of Leonardo's creation, restored in the course of time by many different hands.

The effect of an oil painting is quite different from that of previously used media. Oil lends gloss and depth and a rich glowing tone to the surface; tempera produces softer, more delicate and subdued effects. Fresco and tempera are suited more to the representation of the nonmaterial and spiritual, whereas oil colors effectively express that which is material—the beauties of this world.

For all their advantages, however, oils present certain difficulties. Their slow-drying quality is sometimes a disadvantage, and they are more susceptible than tempera to darkening. Tempera has enjoyed a modern revival that can be seen as part of the reaction against realism in favor of symbolism and expression.

Before using his oils, the painter (or his apprentice) had to grind and mix them. As late as the seventeenth century there were not more than ten colors, among them such oxides as white lead, ocher, and burnt sienna. The most precious and expensive color was ultramarine, made from powdered lapis lazuli. In the middle of the nineteenth century, factory-made colors in tubes became available. Since tubes are easily portable, this development fitted in with the trend of artists to quit their studios and go outdoors to paint directly from nature. Unfortunately, early ready-made paints were often manufactured of poor material like bitumen, and many works—those of the School of Barbizon, for example—are now badly cracked and discolored; compared with them, the paintings of the so-called Primitives of the fifteenth century look fresh and brilliant.

Various techniques were used in applying paints. Dutch masters of the seventeenth century still followed the medieval practice of making a drawing on a canvas and putting in the major lights and shadows. Over this they put successive glazes and then gave the work the final touch with paints mixed with varnishes. The result was a surface of an enamel-like smoothness, the so-called *glacé*. Artists—such as Vermeer and Jan Steen, among others—reached a perfection with this technique that today seems miraculous.

In contrast to this, we find the swift and dashing technique with which other painters gave vent to their emotions by painting the canvas directly, indicating or quickly noting with the brush a figure, a face, or nature. This method, called *alla prima* (because faster, more spontaneous, and less precise), has been described as "writing with a brush" and was used in the sixteenth and seventeenth centuries by Titian, Tintoretto, Rubens, Velázquez, Hals, and Rembrandt. Rubens, for instance, worked with great speed and virtuosity. In his studio whole series of enormous paintings were created—executed by collaborators and apprentices from the master's sketches. One such cycle, now in the Louvre, is comprised of scenes from the life of Marie de Médicis. These paintings, each ten by fifteen feet, were commissioned by Marie for her new palace, the Luxembourg in Paris. Rubens' own studies in oil, of which many hundreds have been preserved, show the playful ease with which he expressed his inexhaustible invention.

In the nineteenth century the same technique led to Impressionism. Whereas the old masters seem to have bent for long periods of time over their work, the Impressionists caught a fleeting moment with swift strokes and indicated only the general forms. They painted rapidly; they had to, for they did not want to portray objects as such, but only the ever-changing play of light upon them. In order to put down their impressions of nature quickly, the Impressionists had the revolutionary notion of painting directly from nature. They left the studio and, working outdoors, recorded the light, airy, sunny colors of nature. After 1870 Claude Monet never worked in his studio, but always painted in a little boat. On the river at Argenteuil he created his sunny Seine landscapes, while his friend Edouard Manet painted him working in his floating studio with his young wife Camille.

The way in which a painter applies the paint to the canvas is characteristic of his method of working, his real signature. The brush work of fast painters can be distinguished clearly even in reproductions. Rembrandt's touch became in time increasingly rough and broad. Van Gogh sometimes applied paint on the canvas directly out of the tube. And the Italian Impressionist Mancini was not satisfied with thick conglomerations of paint; he pushed colored pieces of glass and stone into it to obtain a greater effect of light.

For completely different reasons—to break with the tradition of the *belle peinture* and to achieve a completely new form—the first Cubists, Picasso, Braque, and Gris, added alien elements to their paintings: pieces of newspaper, wood, rope, textiles, and sand. This procedure, called "collage," appeared for the first time around 1910. But the role of the glue pot in the art of painting was a fleeting one, and the founders of Cubism soon returned to more traditional media.

5

Line, Perspective, and Composition

A painting is a composite of lines and colors that together create form. The *line,* the drawing itself, has certainly the oldest right to be considered the basis of the painting. If we return to the beginnings of art, the prehistoric cave paintings, we see that the artist scratched the contours of the animals on the wall before he applied color to his design.

In a work of art, however, the line can have another function than defining contours: it can also express values. Thus, an undulating line has a playful, decorative, and mobile character. Dürer's works or the early paintings of Van Gogh contain angular and stiff lines, while Piet Mondrian's compositions are characterized by geometrical forms. According to the wishes of the painter, lines may express movement or repose; they may be violent, playful, or gentle.

After the painter has made the preliminary drawing on paper, he almost always transfers it to a canvas or panel. On old drawings one sometimes sees that the paper has been divided into squares—evidence that the sketch was to be enlarged. The drawing—showing the contours, the way the clothes fall, and the shadowed parts—is often very detailed, but painting over the drawing on the canvas has to be avoided as much as possible because it also changes the color. Such overpainting is often found in old paintings in the form of slightly darkened areas. In pictures on which the paint has remained transparent, the preliminary drawing is often still visible underneath, as for example in Lucas van Leyden's "Last Judgment."

Some painters make only a rough sketch showing the main lines of the composition. For them, the form is determined not by the line but by the color or, better still, the painting material. The paint itself indicates the form. This method, the *alla prima,* requires a steady hand and great accuracy. Among the pictorial painters who delineated by means of color were Frans Hals, Velázquez, Rubens (in his oil-paint sketches), Titian, Rembrandt, and, in the nineteenth century, Delacroix, the Impressionists, and Cézanne. In contrast to them are the painters who work primarily as draftsmen.

Many artists to whom the line was of first importance worked in the early Renaissance—Mantegna, Botticelli, and Carlo Crivelli, to mention only a few. The Baroque period, which followed, was mainly "painterly" (a term first used by the art historian Heinrich Wölfflin to mean the concentration upon mass rather than upon line), but the French Neoclassicists, David and Ingres, returned at the beginning of the nineteenth century to the linear style. Ingres used to tell his pupils that the drawing was the main thing and that a well-drawn work was always painted well enough.

The contrast between Ingres, a master of line, and his contemporary Delacroix, a master of color, is a classic one. Yet, when we look at paintings by Ingres, we see at once that color has not been neglected; and, when we examine works by Delacroix, we notice his careful attention to drawing. In his *Journal,* which records so many stimulating thoughts on the art of painting, Delacroix wrote in 1856:

> The first lines with which a good painter indicates his thoughts already contain everything which makes his work attractive. A few strokes with pen or pencil on paper already give an idea of the whole painting. The sketch is the possibility which painting has and which music and poetry do not have. Through its strong, clearly indicative contour, a sketch can have the same value as the most complicated composition with figures.

To Delacroix then the purpose of the line was to convey the thought of the painter.

Colorful paintings appeal mainly to the emotions; strongly linear paintings have an intellectual character. Line and color, however, are by no means mutually exclusive. With Delacroix, as with Titian, Rubens, Rembrandt, and Vermeer, we do not know which to admire more, the beautiful color or the masterly drawing. Likewise the works of Van Gogh, Gauguin, and Toulouse-Lautrec emphasize, equally, strong color and strong drawing.

The Impressionists and Cézanne denied the existence of the line. They declared that lines do not exist in nature and what we call lines are no more than borders of color planes. The three planes of the cube, for example, can be seen not only as a construction of lines surrounding the planes but also as three planes of color. The Impressionist Monet saw nature exclusively as color, and Cézanne, who went even further, ignored perspective and suggested space by modulations of color.

Perspective is the projection of objects in space, as seen by the eye, onto a plane. During the centuries in which the reproduction of visual reality was one of the goals of painting, especially the fifteenth to the eighteenth centuries, perspective was an important science. Painters of landscapes and interiors, such as Canaletto, were especially fond of creating the illusion of space by means of lines. This illusion, however, could also be attained by alternating color, tone, light, and shadow. The contrast between the two methods can be seen in the different techniques of two Italian painters of the eighteenth century, both masters of the Venetian *veduta* ("view"): Guardi, who worked with light and shadow, and Canaletto, a draftsman who depended largely upon lines to gain his effects.

During the Middle Ages painters ignored perspective. Yet, like us they must have observed that parallel lines seem to approach each other in the distance and that objects seem smaller the farther away from us they are. The medieval artist painted not what he saw but what he believed in. His purpose was neither the imitation of nature nor the re-creation of visual reality and depth. Thus, the Renaissance artists were not necessarily correct in considering medieval painting primitive simply because medieval painters did not apply the rules of perspective. Now, many modern artists, such as Klee, do not choose to make use of it—though they know the principles well.

With the Renaissance there was a greater preoccupation with earthly reality, and artists threw themselves into the study of perspective with enthusiasm. Giorgio Vasari, the first art historian (author of the famous *Vite,* a book about the "lives of the most excellent painters, sculptors, and architects"), tells us about Paolo Uccello, an Italian painter who knew no greater pleasure than to submerge himself in difficult problems of perspective. Once, when he was working late into the night and his wife asked him to come to bed, Uccello is said to have answered, "Oh, che dolce cosa e questa prospettiva!" ("Oh, a sweet thing is this perspective!")

The mathematical laws governing perspective were probably discovered by Brunelleschi, architect of the dome of Santa Maria del Fiore Cathedral in Florence, and applied by Uccello and Piero della Francesca. These men made perspective a science henceforth considered indispensable for artists. Painters north of the Alps also worked on perspective—Jan van Eyck empirically, and Albrecht Dürer scientifically.

Once the laws of perspective had been fully mastered in Italy, they became a means of composition, leading the eye to the focal point of the painting. Leonardo da Vinci in his "Last Supper" used symmetry and perspective to direct the eye toward one central point: the head of Christ. The head is at the center of the painting and is also the "vanishing point" for the perspective. In this, the mechanical devices of composition and perspective are so related to the subject as to create a psychological and pictorial unity. Paolo Veronese used the same method in this "Marriage at Cana," as did Raphael, though less spectacularly, in his "Disputà."

The way an artist distributes lines and color to create unity is called *composition.* Art is order, and every painting has a certain structure, equilibrium, and balance. Still, the organization may not always be obvious. Often the painter, wary of stiffness and order, has erased its traces as much as possible. Northern paintings of the sixteenth and early seventeenth centuries, from Pieter Bruegel to Hendrick Avercamp, often show a multitude of incidents which, taken together, establish a unity. Bruegel's "Children's Games," "Flemish Proverbs," and "Census in Bethlehem" are only a few examples. Details of these incidents can be enjoyed for their completeness and are often reproduced. In paintings from the Baroque period, however, there is an uninterrupted stream of movement through the work, and each and every detail becomes dependent on the whole.

Composition can be either symmetrical or asymmetrical. In symmetrical paintings an imaginary central axis in the middle of the painting divides it into similar halves. This is done most rigorously in the Byzantine mosaics and less severely in such works as "The Madonna of the Canon van der Paele" by Van Eyck, the "Primavera" by Botticelli, and the "Sistine Madonna" by Raphael. Many medieval paintings show Mary and the Child in the middle of the picture with saints on each side. Usually this picture is a triptych, consisting of a centerpiece and two wings—an arrangement that further reinforces symmetry. One of the favorite elements of composition in the Renaissance was the triangle—used, for example, by Raphael in his Madonnas. From the solid base of the pyramid form, the eye is drawn to the culminating point. The pyramid expresses stability, since its center of gravity is in the middle. In the period following the Renaissance, Baroque artists, favoring asymmetrical paintings, often composed along the diagonal. The diagonal expresses movement, and the center of gravity in such a painting is eccentric. Whereas the symmetrical form of composition is static, the asymmetrical is dynamic. This does not mean that a dynamic composition has no equilibrium. Equilibrium is a matter more of feeling than of geometry. A painting can have the static equilibrium of a Van Eyck, or the dynamic equilibrium of a Rubens. A one-way movement, however, would destroy the equilibrium. A painting by Rubens or Seurat maintains its equilibrium only because the diagonal movement has been balanced by counterdiagonals or other counterforces.

Artists have often looked for an ideal proportion or mathematical relationship representing complete harmony. In antiquity the ideal proportion was well known as the *sectio aurea* ("Golden Section" or "Golden Mean") and was given a high aesthetic and even a mystical value. Actually an irrational number, the *sectio aurea* can be expressed roughly by the proportions 3 to 5, 5 to 8, or 8 to 13. The proportions in Gothic cathedrals, for example, are based on the *sectio aurea*. In typography the relationship between the printed part of the page and the whole page was often governed by the *sectio aurea,* and historians have shown that proportions in works by Raphael, Titian, and Velázquez, among others, were based on the *sectio aurea.** Paintings by Renaissance artists such as Leonardo da Vinci and Albrecht Dürer show that these masters also thoroughly investigated such mathematical relationships.

The emphasis of this chapter has been on the line. As large a role, and in certain periods an even larger one, has been played by color and the effects of light and dark that it creates. We shall, therefore, now turn our discussion to the role of color in painting.

* If a line is divided into two parts in such a way that the smaller has the same proportion to the larger that the larger has to the whole [a/b = b/(a + b)], then the line is said to be divided according to the *sectio aurea.* The mathematical construction is as follows: Construct a perpendicular at B half as long as AB. Connect A with C. With C as center and BC as radius swing an arc cutting AC at D. Then with A as center and AD as radius, swing an arc cutting AB at E. The point at E now divides the line AB according to the *sectio aurea.*

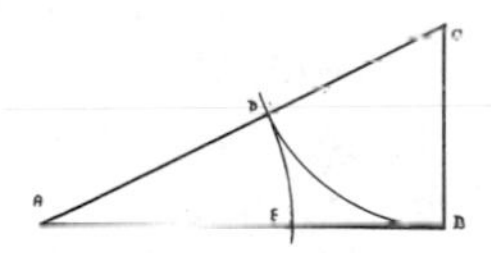

6

Color and Light

Color often plays an important part in the arts of sculpture, drawing, and engraving. Yet, while it adds a charming element, it could have been omitted. The ancient Egyptians, Chinese, and Greeks painted their statues; in the sculpture of post-Renaissance Europe, colors were no longer added. Drawings, too, are sometimes colored, and we find color used in the Japanese woodcuts and the lithographs of Toulouse-Lautrec and Pierre Bonnard. But color is not indispensable to these art forms.

In the art of painting, however, color is an essential element, and in many cases *the one* essential element. We have already seen that the two elements, line and color, vary in importance according to the artist and the period. One artist gives us the color only as something secondary. With another, the painting vanishes if divested of color. Two artists of widely opposing viewpoints, Ingres and Delacroix, have expressed their opinion in the following manner: Ingres asserted that color "decorates a painting, yet it is its servant." Delacroix, however, said: "Colors are music for the eyes, they add themselves like notes. . . . Certain color harmonies create feelings which even music itself cannot hope for." To Ingres color did no more than provide a pleasing touch. To Delacroix color was the primary element of painting, beautiful in itself. Ingres was one of the last painters in the nineteenth century for whom color was only an ornament, and all great colorists among his predecessors provide arguments opposing his point of view. In general we can say that color has with time moved away from a subservient to an equal role, and then to one of almost absolute dominance.

Line, form, and subject make the spectator think; they appeal to his mind. Color, on the other hand, appeals to the emotions, and thus, as Delacroix says, is akin to music. Van Gogh, too, in one of his letters speaks about color as "something which consoles like a piece of music." Music and color even have a similar vocabulary. We talk about the "tone" of a color and about the "color" of a sound. A certain sensitivity is necessary for the enjoyment of color, for color cannot be explained in the same way that composition and subject are explained.

Color appeals to feeling. We associate a "warm" color with fire and earth—red, orange, and brown. "Cool" colors remind us of air, water, and ice—blue, white, and green. Obviously the number of nuances is limitless; shades of yellow and violet, for example, can be either warm or cool. Warm and cool colors can be used in many different ways. Warm colors often give the impression of proximity; cool colors, of distance. Often warm and cool colors are put next to each other for contrast, and a painter may show a preference for one or the other. Some painters who were contemporaries present this striking difference:

Warm	*Cool*
Giorgione	Mantegna
Titian	El Greco
Rembrandt	Saenredam
Ostade	Vermeer
Delacroix	Ingres

Color has many functions in painting. The oldest one is undoubtedly to give a stronger illusion of reality to the subject. Certainly this was the intention of the prehistoric artist when he painted his bisons and wild horses with earth colors that came very close to the actual coloring of the animals.

In the early Middle Ages, on the other hand, colors were not always used realistically. For example, the manner in which color was distributed on the mosaics that decorate the walls of early Christian and Byzantine churches often achieved unrealistic effects. The small pieces of glass, enamel, and stone (tesserae) are not in one plane but have been pressed irregularly into the plaster. The color is never smooth. New facets catch the light all the time, giving a sparkling result of deep blue, emerald green, and ruby red, alternating with the dull white of the marble and the radiance of the oft-used, gold-colored glass. Even more impressive are the color effects of the stained-glass windows in Gothic cathedrals. They receive their color not from the light that shines on them but from the light that passes through them. In the unearthly glow of medieval stained-glass windows, the most striking of which can be seen in the cathedral of Chartres, color has become immaterial and transcendental and no longer represents earthly reality.

A world completely different from that of the glittering mosaics is found in the frescoes of Giotto in the Arena Chapel in Padua. As representations of purely human experience these paintings are much closer to us than the mosaic studies of the heavenly hierarchy. The colors, though subdued as is characteristic of the frescoes, are representational, and images which cover the walls of the chapel in three rows surprise us by their luminosity.

For Giotto and the other Italian painters of the fourteenth century, color is related only indirectly to reality. Tradition determined color usage and its symbolic character. In the altarpiece, "The Annunciation," by Simone Martini, the angel and the lily are white, Mary is wearing a red dress with a blue mantle, and the background is in gold. These are the prescribed colors for a painting of this subject—especially the gold, which is not found as a color in nature. Symbolically, gold reflects through its costliness the heavenly glory. In medieval painting it was often used in the background and for the halos around the heads of saints. Toward the end of the Middle Ages gold appears less and less: Giotto used it in his frescoes only for the halos, not for the backgrounds. Already he was more "modern" than Martini, who reflected the medievalism of Sienesecart; and in his later altarpieces the background consists of landscapes and architecture. In the Renaissance, gold vanished almost completely, although it was still used by "conservative" painters such as Fra Angelico and Carlo Crivelli. In later paintings the gold of the frame may perhaps remind us of the symbolical function of this color, for the frame forms a border between the painting and reality. After the Middle Ages the symbolic use of color gradually disappeared. A strong preoccupation with color as symbol (this time in a highly personal context) emerged only much later with Van Gogh.

The painters of the fifteenth century used few colors and these they kept well apart in closed planes. A red or blue dress would be painted lighter in the light and darker in the shadow, but it remained red or blue and contrasted with an adjacent green or white. In other words, the artists only painted in colors as intense as those in the foreground. No matter how progressive Van Eyck was in his reproduction of light and shadow, he remained conservative in his treatment of local color.

In terms of visual reality, however, local color shows all kinds of gradations (tones) under the influence of light and atmosphere. Colors seen at a distance are much weaker than colors nearby. A surface shows gleams of light, and each color is modified by and receives new values from adjacent colors. During the Renaissance these phenomena were discovered by the Venetians of the sixteenth century. With the Florentine painters, from Botticelli to Michelangelo, the accent was always on line; color was used only to enhance the form. With the great Venetians—Giorgione, Titian, and Veronese—color became important in itself. Titian, especially in his later work, was one of the first great colorists. He did not use color merely to fill a contour; for him it became a personal and emotional "brush writing" that could achieve hitherto unknown effects. This use of color, pioneered by the Venetians, was continued in the seventeenth century by Rubens, Rembrandt, Hals, and Velázquez. In the nineteenth century it was again taken up by Delacroix and Manet.

Artists became increasingly interested in the pictorial effects of the natural fall of light from the beginning of the fifteenth century. With Jan van Eyck began a growing tendency toward chiaroscuro (the contrast between light and shadow). He depicted shadows (Giotto and Martini had already painted body shadows) cast by a source of light outside the painting. As Van Eyck was commencing the "Ghent Altarpiece" the young Florentine painter Masaccio was completing his series of frescoes showing episodes from the life of the apostle Peter, and in one of these there is a scene in which sick people are healed when Peter's shadow falls on them. Earlier painters would have been unable to show this miracle. Still another step forward in the use of light and shadow came when the Haarlem painter Dirk Bouts depicted the phenomena of light in nature—sunrise, dusk, and moonlight—in landscape backgrounds.

Chiaroscuro heightened dramatic expression and was an important means of composition in seventeenth-century Baroque painting. The technique, which had already been explored and used by Titian and Tintoretto, found its fullest expression in the work of Caravaggio, who created striking contrasts of light and dark through simulation of an outside light source, as if his personages were in a cellar and a concentrated beam of light were entering through a high window—a technique called "cellar-light" or "arch-light." Caravaggio had a great influence on the artists of the seventeenth century—on the mediocre ones as well as the great ones, including Rubens, Velázquez, and above all Rembrandt, who made of chiaroscuro a visionary means of expression.

The introduction of an artificial light within a scene, a device that Tintoretto had used earlier, also became popular in the seventeenth century. In his younger years Rembrandt painted money-changers and scientists in dusty rooms, achieving strong light effects from a burning candle. His pupil Gerard Dou repeated this theme in his well-known "Evening School," which was a real tour de force. Later Rembrandt repeatedly painted scenes having artificial lighting and achieved in them some of his greatest expressions, including "The Denial of St. Peter" and the "Conspiracy of Claudius Civilis."

In the seventeenth century the Dutch landscape painters indicated perspective through "tones," the different gradations of local color later called *valeurs* by the French painters of the nineteenth century. Generally speaking, in landscapes dating before and around the year 1600, the painter used a so-called three-color perspective: the foreground was painted in brown hues, the middle ground in green, and the background in blue. Then painters such as Jan van Goyen made great use of "aerial perspective"—the atmospheric effect on colors, causing them to lose strength and intensity the farther they are away from the observer (a technique already employed by Masaccio in his Brancacci Chapel frescoes). By using a slowly diminishing intensity of color, the painter could suggest endless, unlimited space. Indeed, Van Goyen neglected local colors so much in his conquest of space that his paintings sometimes seem almost monochromatic. Later, with Jacob van Ruisdael, Meindert Hobbema, and Aelbert Cuyp, the landscape again became colorful and, at the same time, tones were used to suggest distance.

After the powerful art of the seventeenth-century Baroque, with its great interest in a dramatic range of color and value, eighteenth-century Rococo painters had a lighter touch. The refined colors of Watteau and Fragonard suited the elegant furniture and the light hues of pink, soft blue, light green, and gold of the Louis XV drawing rooms. Many painters, such as Quentin de la Tour, Perronneau, and Jean Liotard, preferred pastels to the heavier oil paints.

Classicism before and after 1800 was not very much interested in color. Pure design based on Greek sculpture was the main thing. Neither the French Barbizon group, nor the School of The Hague (so intensely interested in grayish hues), nor even a great master like Corot added much to the study of color. Seventeenth-century knowledge of color remained intact throughout the eighteenth century.

In the nineteenth century color became truly independent. Artists of earlier centuries had used color partly by intuition and partly by experiment, and now science came to the painter's aid. In 1702 Newton had shown that white sunlight consisted of a number of colors that could be seen if the light were led through a crystal prism. These colors of the rainbow, or of the "spectrum," could be arranged in a circle consisting of red, orange, yellow, green, blue, and violet. Of these six colors, red, yellow, and blue are simple or "primary" colors, which cannot be obtained by mixing. The other three are "secondary" colors: orange is a mixture of red and yellow; green, of yellow and blue; and violet, of blue and red. Colors opposite each other in the circle are called "complementary colors." Thus, the complementary color of red is green (because green contains the two other primary colors); of yellow, violet; and of blue, orange.

Although there are only three primary and three secondary colors, the number of gradations from one color to another is, of course, much larger. Furthermore, the colors of the spectrum are pure—that is to say, not mixed with white or black. By mixing them with white or black we can create an infinite number of shades.

The English landscapists Constable and Turner and the French painter Delacroix were the first artists to utilize scientific principles of color. In 1824 Delacroix sent a large painting representing a scene from the Greek War of Independence, called "The Massacre of Chios," to the annual Paris Salon. Shortly before the opening of the Salon, Delacroix saw a painting by Constable there that struck him by the freshness of its green. Constable had discovered that he could paint a very intense green if he put touches of different greens next to each other instead of painting one even color. Delacroix was so impressed that he took his own painting back and repainted it according to the new principle. In the same way Turner achieved the glittering whiteness of snow by placing different tones of white next to each other.

Once on the trail of the laws of color, Delacroix made another discovery. Having no success in giving sufficient strength to a yellow curtain he was painting, he sent for a carriage to take him to the Louvre in order to study this problem in paintings of others. Chance would have it that a yellow carriage drove up. As Delacroix was on the point of getting in, he noticed that, in the fierce sunlight, the yellow carriage threw a violet shadow. He dismissed the driver, ran back to his studio, and gave the yellow curtain violet shadows. Now the yellow had the needed strength. Delacroix had discovered that a color has its complement for a shadow and that these two colors strengthened each other. Chevreul proved this phenomenon scientifically and called it *contrastes simulantées des couleurs* ("simultaneous contrast of colors").

While other painters achieved shadows by adding black to the local color, Delacroix systematically used the natural contrast between colors to obtain light and shadow. Because his shadows had, therefore, much stronger color, he could put intense reds and blues in the light—something impossible for his contemporaries since their brownish and blackish shadows would not have provided sufficient counterbalance.

Replacing the brown and black in shadows by pure color meant a kind of revolution because the painter henceforth did not reproduce the "plastic volume" of his objects. There had always been some relationship, strong or weak, between painting and sculpture, but the process of freeing painting from plastic influences, begun by Titian, now found its culmination. The Impressionists took their bow in 1874 and painted the world not in its tangible, material reality but as it appeared in colors. They forgot that matter has volume and weight. Everything, even the shadows, became color. Chiaroscuro vanished, and color freed itself from the objects and became truly independent.

Monet and his circle wanted to reproduce natural light in the outdoors, the plein-air. Since their predecessor Constable had already found that a color would lose much of its power when mixed, they used color as much as possible without mixing it, putting it on the canvas in light dabs. Seen from a distance, these dabs melt together into the nuances that the artists wanted. The Neo-Impressionists Georges Seurat and Paul Signac systematized this method by putting colors on the canvas in little dots. The term *pointillism* has been applied to this method of painting.

Monet's dabs of color expressed the vibrating sunlight. Cézanne's colors were more dense and melted together into simple planes. Whereas the Impressionists used the light as the main actor in the painting, Cézanne was not interested in changes of light and shadow. Instead, he built the world of his paintings out of planes of color, which by their modulations express light and space.

Van Gogh's attitude toward color was quite different again. For him color was the means to make visible an idea, a state of the soul. Early in his career he had written, "Color expresses something on its own account." Even then, however, he had not freed himself from "local" color. But in Arles, after his "impressionistic" period in Paris, he no longer used color (or at least not exclusively) to produce natural effects. Color became the "jumping board for the jump above nature." Local color was now only the beginning. For instance, he painted the portrait of an artist friend as faithfully as possible at first; then he intensified the color. "I exaggerate," he explained, "the blonde of the hair to orange, to chrome, to light lemon-yellow. Behind the head, instead of the trivial wall of the room, I paint Infinity, from the richest, deepest blue which I can mix; and this simple combination, the bright blonde head against a rich, blue background, gives an effect as mysterious as a star in the deep sky." Well-known, too, is what Van Gogh wrote about the harsh colors in his painting "The Night Café." They are there, he explained, "to express that this is a place where one can ruin oneself, where one can go mad, or commit a crime."

With Van Gogh color regained the symbolic function it had had in the Middle Ages. But, leaning especially on Delacroix, he often used complementary colors to strengthen each other—as with purple irises against a yellow background. In his most beautiful self-portrait, the one with the pipe and bandages painted after his conflict with Gauguin, he wears a cobalt-blue cap and a green coat. The upper half of the background is orange, the lower half, vermilion. Thus, the painting consists of two pairs of complementary colors which produce a remarkably striking contrast.

Along with the Impressionists and Cézanne and Van Gogh, Paul Gauguin must be mentioned as one of those who freed color from representational restrictions. In his exotic fantasies he painted violet trees and pink and orange fields, using colors to create purely decorative effects.

In the main currents of the twentieth century color is no longer used to portray reality, but rather to express emotional and spiritual values. Both the French *fauves* (wild beasts), among whom Henri Matisse was the main figure, and the German Expressionists, including Franz Marc (who painted red and blue horses and blue deer), used intensified and nonrepresentational colors. With Raoul Dufy, the broadly applied planes of color do not even relate to the outlines of the drawing.

Color reached its greatest importance among Nonobjective painters. Here the effect of the painting depends entirely on the relationship and the tension between color and form, and here painting indeed approaches the most abstract of arts, music. Many of these artists (among them Kandinsky and Delaunay) have drawn attention to that relationship and to the new role of color. In modern Nonobjective painting, color is not only dominant but also completely autonomous.

7

Art as a Mirror of Time, Milieu, and Personality

Every country leaves the imprint of its culture on its art. The artist belongs to a society and mirrors to a great extent the cultural period; in addition, the artist has, like every other human being, the characteristics of personality. As man's ideas about the world change, the language of art, in which the current of human thought is reflected, changes too.

The art characteristic of any period is called the "style" of that period. A certain style may be more or less international, but within it we find great differences which are said to characterize various "schools." The Baroque was the dominant style of seventeenth-century Europe, but Baroque characteristics were much purer in Italian and Flemish art than in Dutch art, which had a more bourgeois character. Dutch Baroque art, in turn, can be subdivided into several schools, including those of Utrecht, Leiden, and Delft.

These differences of nationality and locality are far more noticeable in paintings of earlier centuries than in modern works. Nowadays there is a great exchange of ideas among nations; exhibitions and the stream of art books and magazines have to a large degree eliminated national borders. Another reason for the disappearance of national borders in art is that during the past hundred years most important painters, French and non-French, found their way to Paris, which became the Mecca of modern art.

In a museum a person walking from the Italian to the Flemish or Dutch hall, is immediately struck by the difference in concept;

in one he finds monumental form, whereas in the other he will see careful observation and detail. The Italian concept has been called "idealistic," the Dutch concept, "realistic." The first gives an ennobled image; the latter concentrates on objective reality. Compare a Madonna by Jan van Eyck with one by Raphael, or a portrait by Antonio Moro with one by Titian. Actually the terms "realism" and "idealism" are only relative. Generally speaking, "realism" is concerned with appearance rather than with essence. Such a definition may, however, be misleading. Seventeenth-century Dutch genre painters were realists outwardly, but they painted their intimate domestic scenes from a purely idealistic point of view.

Each country, too, places its peculiar stamp and habit of mind on its art. Spanish art from El Greco to Goya, German art from the days of Dürer, French art of the eighteenth century, and English portrait painting all have, besides the individual traits of the artists, their national characteristics. And although certain periods may evidence similar styles, contemporaries often show striking differences—as, for example, those of the Frenchman Eugène Delacroix and the German Caspar David Friedrich.

When we consider the international aspects of art, we find that one country often assimilates elements from the art of another. In the work of the Northern Mannerists of the sixteenth century we find elements of Michelangelo and Raphael. Likewise, the chiaroscuro of Caravaggio found its way to the Netherlands, Spain, and France. Chardin's still lifes and interiors show touches of Vermeer and Terborch, and portraits by Gainsborough remind us of those by Van Dyck. The English landscapists of the days of Constable and the French painters of Barbizon found their starting point in the art of Ruisdael, Hobbema, and Cuyp; and Barbizon in its turn led to the School of The Hague. One can cite examples almost indefinitely, because influences can always be found. The important question is whether the foreign example has been merely copied or whether it has been absorbed into the personality of the artist.

Still another influence on the character of a painting is the social position of the person who commissioned it. When Rubens worked for a prince, he painted a series of colossal canvases for the decoration of palaces—allegorical and mythological scenes of grandiose and decorative allure. Dutch painters in the seventeenth century, on the other hand, worked for citizens who did not want abstruse allegories or fanciful subjects but who preferred what Fromentin calls *ce qui ressemble* ("that which is recognizable"). Van Dyck and, later, Gainsborough painted portraits for the English nobility; their work has a character quite different from that of the robust portraits of citizens painted by Frans Hals and Cornelis de Vos. But the development of art does not always continue unbroken. When, as happened during the French Revolution, the social structure of a nation suddenly changes, the changes in art have been as abrupt. Before the Revolution, art mirrored the luxury and the light-hearted life of the nobility; afterward it reflected the battle spirit of "La Marseillaise."

Still another characteristic of most paintings is the personality of the artist, an element that became especially significant with the Renaissance. Byzantine art was impersonal, and we do not even ask the names of the artists. Collective thought was then stronger than personality. The medieval painter made himself an interpreter of the common faith, not of himself. He did not even sign his work. That only became customary toward the end of the Middle Ages, after Jan van Eyck. On the frame of a small panel showing St. Barbara with a beautiful Gothic tower being built in the background, we see the words "Johes de Eyck me fecit 1437" ("Jan van Eyck made me in 1437"). From the Renaissance on, however, the personal element in every painting that is not an imitation is unmistakable. Two landscapes, one by Courbet and the other by Corot, leave completely different impressions; one is solid and material, the other poetic and ethereal. The landscapes are not just *painted* by Courbet and Corot, they *are* Courbet and Corot. Nature has been seen here *à travers un tempérament* ("through a temperament").

Of course, mistakes are possible. We are standing in front of a painting we have never before seen and think, "Rubens," or in front of another one, "Picasso from his Cubist days." Then we look in a catalogue and find that we have been wrong. The Rubens turns out to be an early Van Dyck; the Picasso, a Braque. Yet, we were not too far off. The influence of the period and the relationship of master and pupil, or similarity of intentions, may have outweighed the personal elements.

The personal element in the work of an artist changes during his life. Compare, for example, the work of the young with that of the old Rembrandt, or the dark paintings by Van Gogh from his days at Nuenen with the bright-colored ones from St. Rémy, painted only six years later. Who would believe that an impressionistic landscape painted in 1895 and a neo-plastic composition from 1920 were both works of Mondrian. Picasso, too, changed his style often; whenever he mastered a certain mode of expression, he left it behind and tried something else. It is more common, however, that a painter who arrives at a certain style and is successful with it stays with this means of expression for the rest of his life.

If art changes in the course of time, so does the vision we have of it. The Impressionists were mocked or ignored by their contemporaries; but later generations have received their work differently and have praised them. Other painters, such as Meissonier and Alma-Tadema, were among the most admired artists of their own day, but are now almost forgotten. Paulus Potter's "The Young Bull," an example of stark realism, was praised to the skies in the nineteenth century; now it receives scant attention. Still other painters, little known until the middle of the nineteenth century—El Greco, Vermeer, Hercules Seghers, and Matthias Grünewald—have emerged from the darkness of oblivion and are now among the most admired and most coveted masters. For centuries Raphael was the divine artist. But in 1851 Delacroix dared to write in his journal, "Perhaps one day people will think that Rembrandt was a much greater painter than Raphael." And how many art students since Delacroix have not considered Rembrandt the greatest painter of all times!

When the painter and art critic Sir Joshua Reynolds visited the Amsterdam Town Hall in the year 1781, he preferred "The Peace of Münster" by Van der Helst to Rembrandt's "The Night Watch," and many others shared this opinion; yet, when the French writers and art critics Edmond and Jules de Goncourt visited Amsterdam in 1861, they wrote lengthy letters of admiration about "The Night Watch" and considered the "Syndics of the Cloth Guild" the "most amazing piece of art, the most beautiful painting in the world."

Let us take one more example of changing taste in painting. Beginning with the Renaissance, Gothic art was for a long time considered barbaric. Five years after Reynolds made his journey to Flanders and Holland, Goethe began his journey to Italy. Whoever wants to know what the great poet has to say about the art of Giotto will find nothing! Goethe climbed the hill of Assisi, but he did not visit the mighty basilica of St. Francis, on whose walls are scenes from the saint's life painted in Giotto's style. Goethe was interested only in the remains of a Roman temple of Minerva, converted into a church, and he described it enthusiastically. Nor did he visit Siena, the pearl of the Middle Ages. Only with the arrival of Romanticism did people once more turn their attention to the Middle Ages and begin to restore the neglected masterpieces of religious painting. The collection of paintings once belonging to King William II of the Netherlands was auctioned in 1850. A Van Eyck, the "Lucca Madonna," was sold for 3,000 guilders, and a then modern woodland scene by Bernard Koekkoek brought 3,500 guilders. Now, more than a century later, the Koekkoek would bring about the same price (around $1,000), but the Van Eyck is priceless.

Of course, we should not shake our heads about the lack of understanding of previous generations. The future will probably be equally astonished about what we reject or admire.

The creativity of man has produced paintings of almost overwhelming diversity. Nevertheless, works of a particular period and locale, reflecting consistent characteristics, may be said to belong to a given "style." Thus defined, styles provide a convenient means for cataloguing works of art. Dates assigned to those styles may be misleading, however, inasmuch as works may reflect characteristics of more than one period; in addition, a style may have been in the process of formation over a long period of time. In a sense, then, divisions into styles may be deceiving; yet they must be made, for they assist in a description of the development of painting. Their virtue lies in the clarity and order they provide—as we shall see in Part II.

PART II

8

Gothic Art

(Thirteenth, Fourteenth, and Fifteenth Centuries)

From early medieval times the artist had been in the service of the Church. Illuminated manuscripts, symbolic mosaics, and Romanesque murals and architecture served primarily to illustrate the teachings of the Christian religion. According to Gregory the Great, who lived in the sixth century A.D., the purpose of art was to educate and to manifest the glory of God. The basic aim of medieval art, then, was to convey religious truths and to inspire devotion, and its concern was the arrangement of traditional symbols. The Gothic * artist, however, was also involved with rendering his subject full of conviction and emotion, and he achieved a feeling for the religious mysteries by means of symbolic and awe-inspiring means. His concern was indeed the noble expression of the Christian spirit; at the same time he attempted to breathe new life into it.

It was Giotto di Bondone who first broke away from the stylized Byzantine models and with more dramatic freedom of representation set the art of painting in motion. His influence on later Italian painting was profound. With the brothers Limbourg, and with Jan van Eyck and other Flemish painters of the fifteenth

* The word *Gothic* has nothing to do with the Goths—a Teutonic race which moved into Italy during the fifth century A.D. The name was an epithet by the first art historian Vasari to describe the period of art which preceded the "enlightened" era of the Renaissance. People unable to appreciate the ideals and beliefs of the Middle Ages thought of medieval art as cruel and barbaric, and Vasari summarized this opinion when he wrote that Gothic art was "invented by the Goths after these had ruined the buildings of antiquity, and after the architects had perished in the wars. . . . God preserve all countries from this way of thinking and building."

century, a new and growing impulse can be discerned—a current that did not rebel against religious thought but merely wanted to show the beauty of earthly realities: scenes of human activity and landscapes. In time Gothic art gradually became more humanistic in its portrayal of human beings and more realistic in presentation. Finally, in the Renaissance, this worldly aspect gained the ascendancy.

The main schools important to the development of Gothic painting are: (1) Italian art in Florence and Siena during the thirteenth and fourteenth centuries, with Giotto as its greatest representative, (2) miniatures in the French and Burgundian courts at the end of the fourteenth and the beginning of the fifteenth centuries, (3) early Flemish painting in the fifteenth century, best known for its founder and master, Jan van Eyck, and (4) late Gothic art in France and Germany.

ITALIAN ART IN FLORENCE AND SIENA

At the close of the thirteenth century the North had not brought the art of painting to the level of excellence prevailing in architecture and the plastic arts. Gothic churches with their tenuous structure and openwork walls offered little space for large wall paintings, and the climate did not favor them either. In council chambers and palaces, ornate tapestries were much more popular, and in cathedrals the rows of high stained-glass windows were filled with rich color patterns.

In Italy things were different. There, Gothic architecture was rare. In order to preserve coolness and shade in the sunny climate, churches were provided with only small windows. Italian churches had, therefore, wide walls that provided space for large frescoes, and these gradually began to replace the mosaics.

The most noble representative of fresco painting is the Florentine *Giotto di Bondone* (1276?–1337). With Giotto the hieratic quality and convention of the Byzantine style gave way to action, to the expression of purely human emotions in response to the natural aspect of things, and to the first hesitant steps toward perspective. It has been said that the art of painting begins with Giotto—an art which we immediately recognize as such aside from all archeological interests. Giotto's art satisfies our modern feel-

Fig. 1—*Mary and Child enthroned between John and Mark.* **Mosaic dating from the thirteenth century. San Marco, Venice. (Photo: Alinari)**

ings for beauty and humanity, and to understand and appreciate it nothing else is needed than that feeling for beauty and humanity. Giotto can, therefore, well be called a pioneer of a new tradition.

In reality the new expression in Giotto's frescoes was part of the spirit of his own time. In the thirteenth century there had been a growing reaction against the majestic and inaccessible Byzantine religious symbolism (see Fig. 1). Christ, Mary, and the saints of the Church were seated, like royalty, high above the heads of the believers. People longed for a more human and intimate relationship with religious figures and the realities of their faith. St. Francis of Assisi and his disciples stopped using Latin; they spoke to the people in the simple words of the vernacular, repeating what they found in the Gospels. Now, for the first time, people heard the story of the Mother and the Child in the manger and of the kings bearing gifts from faraway countries. Mary, formerly thought of mainly as the Queen of Heaven, became the *Donna úmile,* the humble woman. Divine personages descended, so to speak, from the high walls of the church and mixed with the believers.

Giovanni Cimabue, Giotto's master, was the first to move away from the Byzantine tradition, although he was still strongly influenced by it. According to Vasari, Giotto alone revived that art which turns to nature "and brought it to such a form as could be called good." It was Giotto who finally overthrew the old tradition. Using the new and more intimate style, he and his disciples painted scenes from the life of St. Francis many times over. Some of their most famous works are in the Santa Croce in Florence and in the San Francesco Chapel in Assisi.

Giotto's most famous cycle can be found in Padua in the Arena Chapel, so named because it stands within an old Roman arena. Donated by Enrico Scrovegni, a rich citizen, the chapel was built to atone for the crimes of Enrico's father, an infamous usurer (who is mentioned in the seventeenth canto of Dante's *Inferno*). Around 1305 Giotto painted on the walls of this chapel a series of thirty-six scenes from the lives of Mary and Christ. These scenes present the story of Christian salvation, beginning with the birth of Mary and ending with the "Last Judgment," which is painted above the entrance. The cycle should be looked at in thoughtful concentration and viewed as a story in pictures. Each episode is moving in its simplicity and clarity of expression, its emotion, and its spiritual tension. In the famous "Kiss of Judas," for example, Giotto creates, in a few strong and comprehensive lines, the contrast between good and evil, between the pure and the guilty conscience, as revealed by the faces of Jesus and Judas.

When we look at the "Lamentation over the Body of Christ" (Fig. 2), we are moved by the expressions and attitudes of deep sorrow shown by those surrounding the body. The angels descending like doves and the two women in the foreground with their backs to us partake in the mourning. The figures, faces, and clothes are sketched in simple lines and the surrounding scenery is only summarily indicated. No details distract the onlooker from his participation in this mournful scene. In the simple but carefully executed composition there are two groups of unequal

Fig. 2—Giotto di Bondone: *Lamentation over the Body of Christ. Ca.* 1305. Arena Chapel, Padua. (Photo: Alinari)

size, linked by Christ's horizontal body. To the left we see the smaller group, consisting of plaintive women, with the grieving mother bending over her son. To the right we see a larger group, on the outside of which are Magdalene, seated, Joseph of Arimathea carrying the linen in which the body will be wrapped, and Nicodemus.

In this work there are several new elements. One is the increased illusion of depth. Whereas Byzantine artists had arranged their figures in one plane, Giotto achieved the effect of space through the volume and placement of the figures, especially in the two seated in the foreground. The composition also departs from tradition. The figure of Christ is not in the center; rather, John, the youngest and most beloved disciple, stands there with

Fig. 3—SIMONE MARTINI: *The Annunciation*. 1333. Uffizi Gallery, Florence.

outspread arms, showing more intense sorrow than the others. Nevertheless, the head of Christ is the central point of the composition. All eyes, all attitudes, and even the wall of rock that crosses the scene diagonally, are directed toward it.

In Giotto we sense a spirit of innovation. Compared with him, his contemporaries in the nearby town of Siena were still tied to Byzantine tradition. Even today, Siena represents the Middle Ages, whereas Florence is the town of the Renaissance. Giotto's contemporaries, such as Simone Martini and the brothers Lorenzetti, concentrated mainly on fine paintings of small size, on Madonnas, saints, and religious scenes portrayed against gold backgrounds. Instead of Giotto's drama, we find style, elegance, and charming colors enhanced by the gold.

Simone Martini (1285?–1344), one of Giotto's most important contemporaries, was a courtier and lived for many years at the papal court of Avignon, where he was a friend of the poet Petrarch. His softly radiant work reminds us of the Persian miniatures that were painted in the same century.

His most beautiful work, "The Annunciation" (Fig. 3), portrays the angel Gabriel bringing Mary the glad tidings. The angel wears a white robe; Mary has a blue one over a red dress. The two figures are separated by the symbolic vase of lilies, above which the Holy Spirit hovers in the form of a dove. These are all painted on a background of gold foil. Timidly, Mary draws back from the angel, whose lifted wings and billowing coat show that he has just descended from the skies. Mary's body has no volume; it consists of a fine melodious play of lines, an S-shaped, Gothic arabesque. The figures are gracious and refined and infused with courtly spirit. On the two small wings of this painting, set in a rich Gothic frame, are the patron saints of Siena. The frame, containing medallions with the prophets of the Old Testament announcing the birth of Christ, completes the work.

MINIATURES IN THE FRENCH AND BURGUNDIAN COURTS

Whereas Italian painting began with murals, painting of the North began with the miniatures in illuminated manuscripts.

Italian panel paintings retained on a smaller scale the monumental scope of murals. Northern paintings of the fifteenth century seem like enlarged miniatures.

The art of manuscript illumination was developed in monasteries and at first stayed completely within the religious tradition. This art was highly realistic. The drôleries along the manuscript edges show a sense of worldly humor and whimsical fantasy. The illustrations also depict many natural objects: flowers, birds, and animals of all kinds. In the beginning of the fourteenth century the art of manuscript writing was removed from the writing rooms of the monasteries and placed in the hands of laymen. From then on, worldly elements assumed a greater role in the illustrations: subjects began to be treated realistically; man could be seen more or less as an individual; landscapes received a natural treatment, with perspective and depth; and the gold and decorative backgrounds vanished. The transition from symbolism to realism had begun.

This fine and courtly art was meant for the happy few and flowered unexcelled at the splendid courts of Philip of Burgundy in Dijon and of his uncle, the Duc de Berry, in Bourges. The most beautiful manuscripts known, from the beginning of the fifteenth century, were produced here by the three brothers *Pol, Jan,* and *Hermann Limbourg,* the famous book illustrators from Nijmegen.

The masterpiece *Très Riches Heures* in Chantilly, mostly the work of Pol Limbourg, contains prayers and a calendar of the days of the saints in which miniatures are drawn for each month. In these pages a love of nature has suddenly awakened. With an abundance of clearly seen details and in a fresh and original way, Limbourg has portrayed the seasons with snow scenes, woods, farmlands, the wine harvest, the hunt, and gastronomical pleasures. In the background, against a deep blue sky, rise the high towers and pinnacles of French castles of old Louvre, Vincennes, and Poitiers.

The "October" miniature (Fig. 4) depicts a scene under the smoke of Paris where peasants are harrowing and sowing the winter corn. In a field already sown with grain, a scarecrow in the form of an archer protects the seed from the crows and magpies that can be seen in the left foreground. In the background

Fig. 4—Pol Limbourg: *October*. Miniature from the *Très Riches Heures*. 1413–16. Musée Condé, Chantilly. (Photo: Giraudon)

flows the Seine, with its willows, rowboats, and washerwomen. Beyond the river, Parisian citizens promenade along the river bank at the foot of the mighty wall surrounding the high-towered Louvre castle, the predecessor of the present-day palace. This medieval world is still circumscribed. Walls and towers limit the field of vision. The vast panoramas and limitless space of the landscapes by Van Goyen and Ruisdael were still far off.

Most of the pages of one famous illuminated manuscript were destroyed in 1904 in the fire at the library of Turin (the surviving pages are now kept in Milan). Fortunately, good photographic reproductions had been made of the destroyed pages. The scenes of the landing of Count William V on the dunes of Zeeland and, below it, a Netherlands landscape with a hazy horizon—a completely modern drawing—are well known. These pages, probably done by Jan van Eyck, went even further in developing pure perspective, feeling for space, and atmosphere.

EARLY FLEMISH PAINTING

With Jan van Eyck began a glorious succession of painters, usually called the "Primitives," which included masters from the Northern and Southern Netherlands. In the fifteenth century, Southern Netherlands (now part of Belgium) consisted of Flanders and the Duchy of Brabant—possessions of the House of Burgundy, which formed a political unity with the Northern Netherlands (Holland and Zeeland). The chief activity in painting occurred in the South, in the powerful Flemish towns of Ghent and Bruges, and, to a lesser degree, in the Brabantian towns of Louvain and Brussels. Masters from the other districts, Holland and Zeeland, streamed to these centers.

The name "Primitives" is obviously inappropriate. Indeed, this late-Gothic art shows an almost incredible technical perfection and ingenuity. Increasingly realistic forms were given the sacred images to enhance the viewer's devotion. Thus, a painter would show the angel Gabriel announcing the coming birth of Christ to Mary in a Flemish room with Gothic furniture. On the mantelpiece he placed a little picture of St. Christopher, a giant, who according to myth carried the Christ Child across the river. The anachronism was intentional and heightens the emotional appeal. One panel may contain several episodes from the same story and can be read as if it were a book. Rooms and buildings were not constructed according to the scientific principle of perspective; parallel lines have not one but several vanishing points. In those days the realistic reproduction of the visible world was just beginning to concern the artist.

The Primitives concentrated on religious scenes and portraits. Their subjects reside in an atmosphere of piety with folded hands and devout expressions. The altarpieces are usually triptychs, composed of a middle scene with two side panels, which are also decorated on the back and can be closed. Thus a total of five paintings form the whole, both as a composition and as a story. The polyptych—for example, the famous one by Van Eyck in Ghent or that by Bouts in Louvain—is more rare. Altarpieces generally bear portraits of the rich citizens or prominent church people who ordered the works and donated them to the church. The donor, often surrounded by his wife and children, is kneeling, and his patron saint may be present also.

The saints on altarpieces can be recognized by symbols of miracles they performed or by the instruments of their deaths as martyrs. As a source for these symbols, Gothic painters used the *Golden Legend,* a famous collection of legends and lives of the saints compiled by the thirteenth-century Italian bishop and writer Jacobus de Voragine. The *Golden Legend* was early translated into the vernacular and was one of the most widely read books of the Middle Ages. The following examples are but a few of the well-known saints and their identifying attributes:

John the Baptist—a staff and a lamb (which refer to Christ as the lamb of God).

Mary Magdalene—a vase with salve (with which she anointed the feet of Christ).

Paul—a sword ("And take the helmet of salvation and the sword of the Spirit, which is the word of God").

Peter—a key ("And I will give unto thee the keys of the kingdom of heaven").

St. Barbara—a tower (in which she was imprisoned).

St. Catherine—a broken wheel and a sword (a symbol of her martyrdom).

St. Cecilia—an organ (symbol of her love of music).

St. George—as a knight killing a dragon with his lance.
St. Jerome—a lion (symbol of his life as a hermit in the desert).
St. Martin—as a warrior on his horse with a beggar at his feet, to whom he gives half of his coat.

The Gothic artists of the Netherlands did not sign their paintings, and we have to depend for their names on the testimony of contemporaries, on tradition, and on the *Schilderboeck* (a collection of biographies of painters written in 1604 by Karel van Mander, a Dutch painter and writer). Such is the authority of the *Schilderboeck* that in 1952 the Rijksmuseum of Amsterdam bought a newly discovered triptych that could be identified as one by Lucas van Leyden because it was mentioned in the book as his work. The critics, of course, are not always in agreement.

During the fifteenth century five great masters worked in the Flemish Netherlands: Jan van Eyck, Rogier van der Weyden, Dirk Bouts, Hugo van der Goes, and Hans Memling. (Some would include Hubert van Eyck, but his fame is based only upon an inscription, probably written much later, on a Flemish altar calling him the older brother of Jan van Eyck and his "superior in art.") Of the five known master artists, only Hugo van der Goes from Ghent is probably of Flemish descent. Van Eyck came from Maeseyck in Limbourg; Rogier van der Weyden from Doornik; Dirk Bouts from Haarlem in the northern Netherlands; and Hans Memling from the district of Mainz. Nevertheless, because of their similar surroundings, the political unity existing at that time, and their common view of life, the differences in their origins did not significantly affect their paintings.

At the beginning of Netherlandish Gothic art, we suddenly and unexpectedly find a great altarpiece in the St. Bavon Church in Ghent, a polyptych completed in 1432 by *Jan van Eyck* (1390?–?1441). The "Ghent Altarpiece" (Fig. 5–5a), showing on the middle panel the "Adoration of the Lamb," has remained the mightiest creation of fifteenth-century Netherlandish art. The plasticity of the design, the sparkling, jewel-like richness of color, and the expression of textures are unsurpassed. The whole "Ghent Altarpiece" consists of twenty panels—twelve when opened, eight when closed—summing up the Gothic idea of the unity of heaven and earth. Only one thing is missing in Van Eyck's concept of the world—an image of Hell. This, however, was once depicted on

Fig. 5—JAN VAN EYCK: Middle panels and the *Adoration of the Lamb* from the *Ghent Altarpiece*. Completed 1432. St. Bavon Church, Ghent. (Copyright A.C.L. Brussels)

Fig. 5a—JAN VAN EYCK: Left and right panels from the *Ghent Altarpiece*.
(Copyright A.C.L. Brussels)

the base (predella) on which the altarpiece rested so that the wings could be opened and closed. Originally painted in water colors, it has since been lost.

Although the subjects of these paintings are well within the Gothic tradition, the bold realism is something new. It is expressed with particular force in the nude figures of Adam and Eve and the portraits of the Ghent donors, Jodocus Vijdt and his wife. Also new are the flowing form and the power and transparency of the color, which result from the "revolutionary" technique of oil painting and the way in which Van Eyck saw the people whose portraits he painted. They appear sharply and strikingly as individuals, not as anonymous types. Already the artist has freed himself from the spirit of the Middle Ages. He has become conscious of himself as an individual and has depicted his fellow man in the same way. This is one of the most essential traits of the spirit of the Renaissance. A beautiful illustration of this spirit is Van Eyck's "Giovanni Arnolfini and his Wife." The solemn figures of this pair are shown in the intimate atmosphere of a home, a scene which even Vermeer did not paint with more concentration.

In 1436, a few years after his "Ghent Altarpiece," Jan van Eyck painted "The Madonna of the Canon van der Paele" (Fig. 6). This composition is purely symmetrical. Exactly in the center we see Mary and the Child under a baldachin. The Mother and Child were probably painted from live models, for they are real and very corporeal when compared with those by Simone Martini, with their elegant play of lines. To the right we see the kneeling donor, the Canon Joris van der Paele, whose myopic, fat, wrinkled face Van Eyck has observed with great sharpness. The interior looks like a chapel or the choir of a church, with low, marble pillars carrying Roman arches. Although the perspective is still not completely correct, the illusion of space has been given in a masterly fashion. The rich materials—the Persian rug in front of Mary's throne and the tiles of stone, glass, and metal—are all drawn with unfailing precision of texture. In everything, we feel a love for what *is,* and we sense the care given the smallest detail, while, at the same time, the diverse elements are shaped into a unified whole through the skillful use of composition, light, and the effects of color—achieved

Fig. 6—JAN VAN EYCK: *The Madonna of the Canon van der Paele.* 1436. Communal Museum, Bruges. (Copyright A.C.L. Brussels)

mainly by the beautiful ultramarine blue and gold-brocade of the bishop's cope and miter, by the red in Mary's cloak, and by the white in the canon's surplice.

Once the pictorial qualities of this masterpiece have been enjoyed, several questions still remain for the spectator who is no expert in medieval iconography. Who is the knight in shining armor to the right of Canon van der Paele, and who is the solemn figure in bishop's clothes on the other side, carrying a wheel with burning candles? The knight is St. George (in Flemish, St. Joris), a Roman officer who, according to legend, killed a man-eating dragon in Cappadocia; because of his name he was the patron saint of Joris van der Paele. The altarpiece was painted for the St. Donatus Church (which no longer exists) in Bruges and, therefore, we see also the patron of the church, St. Donatus, once Bishop of Arezzo, whose attribute is the wheel with the five burning candles. St. George politely lifts his helmet and introduces his protégé to the Virgin and Holy Child.

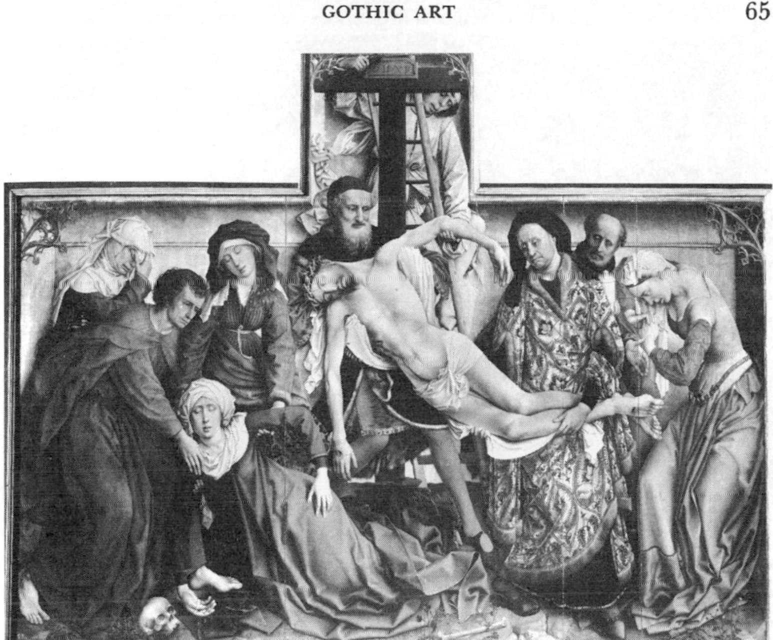

Fig. 7—ROGIER VAN DER WEYDEN: *Descent from the Cross. Ca.* 1435. Prado, Madrid.

Unlike the brilliant discoverer Jan van Eyck, whose work strongly influenced the painting of the portrait, the interior, the landscape, the still life, and the nude, *Rogier van der Weyden* (1399?–1464) from Doornik represented the *via media.* Doornik was a town of sculptors and Van der Weyden's father was one of them. For this reason, perhaps, Van der Weyden achieved a style of magnificent, balanced composition in plastic and monumental groups, which sometimes, as in his famous "Descent from the Cross" (Fig. 7), reminds us of sculptured reliefs.

With extreme care the scene of "Descent from the Cross" is built into a harmonious whole in which every figure has its complement. The outlines of the body and arms of Christ correspond to those of the swooning Mary. The three figures on the left (St. John and the two Marys) have their counterparts in the three on the right (Nicodemus, Mary Magdalene, and an unknown man who carries her vase with salve). Both groups are

Fig. 8—DIRK BOUTS: *The Last Supper*. *Ca.* 1465. St. Peter's, Louvain, Belgium. (Copyright A.C.L. Brussels)

linked by the diagonals of the bodies of Christ and his mother. To the left of the cross, opposite young Simon of Cyrene on the ladder, is the bearded Joseph of Arimathea. In spite of the methodical arrangement, the painting expresses considerable drama and expression of feeling.

Dirk Bouts (1410?–1475) established himself as a town painter in Louvain, in the province of Brabant. He developed a quiet and subdued style, sometimes labeled as "Dutch." Whereas the Fleming Van der Weyden was emotional and dramatic, Bouts was a keen observer of nature. He placed his elongated, stiff, yet very much alive Gothic figures within the atmosphere of interiors and landscapes. His most famous works are the two large scenes of the legendary "Justice of Otto" (now in Brussels) painted for the town hall in Louvain and the altarpiece of "The Last Supper" (Fig. 8) for St. Peter's Church in the same town. What one encounters above all in the latter painting, which has as its setting a Gothic room, is the striking perspective. The four side panels show scenes of miraculous meals from the Old Testament, which impress us with their strong sense of space and atmosphere and with the unity of the figures and the landscapes. The desert scene with the rain of manna and the beautiful sunset is especially dramatic. Here we find the same "modern" trend as in the previously mentioned miniatures of Pol Limbourg and Jan van Eyck.

Hugo van der Goes (1440?–1482) was another of the great fifteenth-century artists. He, more than anyone else, shared Jan van Eyck's love of realism. But we find in his work a strong emotion and spiritual unrest which contrast with the serenity and calm of Van Eyck. In his youth, Van der Goes withdrew from the community to live in the Red Cloister near Brussels and there, stricken by a mental illness, this gentle artist died at the age of fifty-two. In all his work Van der Goes shows a strong mystical tendency and a sensitivity for space, for landscape, and for flowers.

His most famous work, the great "Portinari Altarpiece," was commissioned by the Italian Tommaso Portinari, the representative of the Medici banking house in Bruges. More than eighteen feet wide when opened, it is the largest altarpiece ever painted in

Fig. 9—HUGO VAN DER GOES: Middle panel of the *Portinari Altarpiece. Ca.* 1476. Uffizi Gallery, Florence. (Photo: Alinari)

the Netherlands. On the middle panel, "The Adoration of the Shepherds" (Fig. 9), we see the Nativity; the shepherds approach from the right to worship the Child. Here, Van der Goes introduces not only the element of movement but also the peasant element. The faces of these people are beautifully portrayed. Even the painters of peasants of later centuries, such as Bruegel and Millet, did not do better. There is a tender glow upon the rough, stubbly faces as they gaze upon the Child, who, lying motionless within the radiance, is more a symbol than a living being. Mary kneels within the magic circle formed by Joseph, the ox and the ass, and the four groups of angels and shepherds. In the foreground, which remains free so as not to obstruct the view of the Child, the circle is closed by a sheaf of straw, a colored vase with a lily and irises, and a glass vase with columbines. In contrast to the round composition of the central panel, the side panels are composed vertically and thus provide a suitable frame.

They show the portraits of the donor with his wife and children, dominated by the imposing presence of their patron saints.

The strong emotional and spiritual quality of Van der Goes's figures are most pronounced in another work, "The Death of the Virgin," in the grief-stricken faces of the apostles. The blank, staring faces of these men, each lost in his own sorrow, show us, more than in any other work by Van der Goes, something of the mind of the painter himself.

Hans Memling (1430?–?1495), one of the last masters of the Middle Ages, was neither a discoverer nor a reviver; rather, he carried on in softened and refined forms the work of Van Eyck and Van der Weyden. His paintings are lowly and naïve, often more superficial than those of his predecessors, but moving by their still truly medieval piety, as in the triptych of the "Marriage of St. Catherine." One can learn much about Memling by visiting the Chapter Room of the Hospital of St. John in Bruges, where his spirit endures in a long series of works and where we find the mild, dreamy atmosphere of the once famous trading center of Bruges, which in Memling's time, in the waning days of the Middle Ages, had already passed its zenith.

Gerard David (1460?–1523), Memling's successor in Bruges, came from the little town of Oudewater in Holland. It is believed that he became the pupil of another great master from the same town, Albert van Ouwater, only one of whose paintings has been identified with certainty—"The Resurrection of Lazarus." David was not an innovator; rather, his work sums up the late Gothic style in which the religious spirit is reflected in intricacy of detail and refinement. His great triptych of the "Baptism of Christ in the Jordan" (Fig. 10) is striking. Here the beautiful landscape with woods and a river is no mere background. The ivy and ferns, the violets and the lilies of the valley, the reeds and grasses in the river, and the leaves of the trees belong in the scene and are painted with the care of a botanist.

In the Mauritshuis in The Hague there are two small panels by David with forest views (actually the outer panels removed from an altarpiece triptych, the center panel of which is now in the Metropolitan Museum in New York). They are interesting because they are among the earliest examples of landscapes without figures.

Fig. 10—Gerard David: *Baptism of Christ in the Jordan.* 1507. Communal Museum, Bruges. (Copyright A.C.L. Brussels)

FIG. 11—GEERTGEN TOT SINT JANS: *The Nativity at Night. Ca.* 1490. National Gallery, London. (Reproduced by courtesy of the Trustees, The National Gallery, London)

Sadly, little of the work of the early painters of the Northern Netherlands has been preserved. Protestant iconoclastic outbursts, which raged through the Netherlands in 1566 at the beginning of the long and bloody struggle against Spain, destroyed most of the old church masterpieces—an irretrievable catastrophe for the religious art of the Northern Netherlands. Albert van Ouwater's work, for example, vanished almost completely.

Geertgen tot Sint Jans (1465?–1495), another of Ouwater's pupils, was born in Leiden and later moved to Haarlem, where he lived and painted in the St. John Monastery. Much of his work has disappeared, but one panel—"The Crucifixion"—of his chief work, an altarpiece for the church of the St. John Monastery, has been saved and is now in Vienna. Another work that has been preserved, "The Nativity at Night" (Fig. 11), shows how far ahead of his time Geertgen was. This work depicts for the first time the Nativity presented as a night scene. The light emanating from the Child radiates through the darkness and lights up the faces of Mary and the angels around the cradle. Whereas Memling painted this scene in daylight, using a candle in Joseph's hand to express "night" symbolically, Geertgen's colors actually light up the darkness.

Hieronymus Bosch (1450?–?1516), born in 's Hertogenbosch, introduced a new spirit into painting. With him the old devotion and the traditional subjects, the Madonna and Child, were replaced by the demoniacal and the fantastic—highly personal testimonies of strange dreams and hellish visions. Bosch lived in days of spiritual unrest and confusion, of doubt and disbelief; the Reformation was in the wind, and a year after Bosch's death Luther published his ninety-five theses. The fears that seem to have passed by his contemporary Gerard David were felt intensely by Bosch. The devil was lurking everywhere; fear of hell and damnation became an obsession. In his "Temptation of St. Anthony" and in the painting of his own patron saint, Hieronymus ("St. Jerome"), he identified himself with his subjects—besieged by an army of monstrous, amphibian creatures. Born from demonic and perverse hallucinations, Bosch's creations show great imaginative power. This nightmare world does not seem ridiculous or childish to modern man; rather, it is highly believable in psychological terms. Bosch's art has a hidden power of suggestion that attracts us and stimulates our fantasy.

One of Bosch's smallest but most important works, completed near the end of his life, is the "Prodigal Son" (Fig. 12). It is painted in soft, subdued tones of yellow-gray, gray-blue, and olive-green. In the middle of the panel we see the Prodigal Son homeward bound, emaciated and so ragged that one knee shows

Fig. 12—HIERONYMUS BOSCH: *Prodigal Son. Ca.* 1510. Museum Boymans-van Beuningen, Rotterdam.

through his trousers. He wears one shoe and one slipper, carries a bundle on his back from which a spoon and a cat skin are dangling, and has just emerged from a dilapidated inn called "The Swan." A dog growls at him and a woman behind a window follows him with her eyes; another woman, standing in a doorway, is being caressed by a soldier.

The imaginative qualities of Bosch's work sometimes cause us to overlook the artistic innovations. In the "Prodigal Son" the medieval tramp was shown for the first time in a painting. Bosch was a pioneer, too, in his portrayal of an "impressionistic" landscape which extends wide and billowing in blonde tones under the gray sky toward a hazy horizon.

As a composition, the work is outstanding. The main figure, the Prodigal Son, is on the center line of a circle; by the way he leans forward, he expresses movement. Round paintings, rare in Netherlandish art, were more common in contemporary Italian art, where such a painting was called a *tondo*. Perhaps Bosch intended to raise the work to a symbolic level—to paint the mirror wherein man recognizes himself.

Fifteenth-century Europe had really only two leading schools of art—the Italian and the Flemish. The two influenced each other, but Italy was always one step ahead in the evolution. Later, in the sixteenth century, Italy took undisputed leadership, and the influence of her great masters radiated in all directions.

LATE GOTHIC ART IN FRANCE AND GERMANY

Fifteenth-century French painters were under both Italian and Flemish influences. One master, *Jean Fouquet* (1416?–1480), known especially for his beautiful miniatures, painted the *Heures d' Étienne Chevalier,* similar to *Très Riches Heures* of the Limbourg brothers. (Both works are now in the castle of Chantilly.) For the same Étienne Chevalier, who was treasurer of Charles VII, Fouquet painted a diptych. On one of its panels, now in Berlin, we see a very stylish portrait of Chevalier, with his patron saint, St. Étienne. On the other panel, now in Antwerp, is the Madonna surrounded by red and blue angels. The model for the figure of the Virgin was Charles VII's mistress, Agnes Sorel, who died in 1450 and to whose memory the painting was dedicated.

German painting in the fifteenth century was largely influenced by the Netherlands. Around 1400 *Meister Francke* painted altarpieces for the churches of Hamburg. In the cathedral of Cologne, around 1441, *Stefan Lochner,* a fine artist, painted the "Adoration of the Kings," a triptych set against a golden background;

in Basle, *Konrad Witz* did some pioneering work in landscape painting, as in his "The Miraculous Draught of Fishes"; and in the Tyrol, in the church of the little Austrian town of St. Wolfgang, *Michael Pacher* produced a famous altarpiece, a sculptured shrine with painted panels showing the life of the local saint. Finally, we must mention the painter from Colmar, *Martin Schöngauer,* renowned especially for his beautiful engravings. None of these painters, however, had the prestige of their contemporaries in the Netherlands. They worked in widely dispersed centers, and their works were more provincial and less refined. Their contribution lies above all in that they sometimes achieved a strong and moving spirituality.

9

The Renaissance

(Fifteenth and Sixteenth Centuries)

Historians have generally given the name "Renaissance" to the unparalleled flowering of the arts in Italy during the fifteenth and a large part of the sixteenth centuries. The word "Renaissance" (*Rinascimento,* meaning rebirth) was intended to signify the rebirth of the classical learning of the Greeks and Romans. Certainly the revival of interest in antiquity was important; but, in addition, there were many far-reaching social and intellectual changes. Behind these new interests and changes lay an intellectual self-assertion and self-reliance. It might be better, therefore, to think of the Renaissance as a period seeking freedom from the restrictions of the Middle Ages.

In the Middle Ages painting served the Church and the Christian religion. In the Gothic period, however, there were occasional indications of an increasing interest in earthly reality. At the beginning of the fifteenth century these changes crystallized in Italy. A new concept of the world began to direct the eyes of man away from heaven and down to earth, and in their painting artists gradually moved away from the Byzantine and Gothic styles. It was not that sacred values were suddenly replaced by secular ones, for the Church was still powerful and the age devout. Rather, the new vision of the natural world was an extension of the previous, more circumscribed one.

The Renaissance was a time of discovery. Increased interest in natural phenomena led to many advances in science—which developed peaceably alongside religion, until the open conflict four centuries later at the time of the French Revolution. Anatomy, astronomy, and mathematics were studied; and the architects Brunelleschi and Alberti discovered the laws of perspective.

The new interest in the world and in man was similar to that of antiquity. Even during the Middle Ages a vestigial memory of the classical past survived. The Renaissance was no sudden discovery or revival of antiquity, but it did borrow many elements from it and tried to reconcile Christianity with the culture of the Greeks and Romans. Reason as a guide to life was admitted alongside faith and authority, and man was preoccupied with things human as well as with things divine.

In the *trecento* (fourteenth century), Italian painting gradually moved away from traditional Christian symbolism. *Quattrocento* (fifteenth century) Renaissance art began to employ subjects from Greek mythology and history. Religious subjects, however, did not vanish; on the contrary, the Church remained the patron of art and the commissions she assigned led to some of the most famous creations of the Italian Renaissance. The Renaissance artist, in depicting religious subjects, expressed values different from those of his medieval predecessor; the accent was no longer on transcendental subjects, but on Man, who became the "measure of all things." Fifteenth-century Italy showed one continuous evolution. Perspective was investigated and put on a scientific basis, and problems of harmony, anatomy, and free movement were studied. In essence, the Italian Renaissance meant the true birth of a modern and individual approach to art.

Not until the sixteenth century was the art of the North infused with the Renaissance spirit. Albrecht Dürer, the greatest pioneer figure in Northern Renaissance painting, visited Italy twice and studied the theories current there, particularly as set forth in Leonardo's *Treatise on Painting*. The influence of the Italian Renaissance may be clearly seen in the increasingly ordered, formal structures of Dürer's later works as compared with the rich medieval patterns and detail of his early productions. Two Netherlandish painters, contemporary with Dürer, had contributed to the stirring Renaissance spirit in the North. Bosch had penetrated the nether regions of human nature, masterfully delineating man's basest as well as his noblest impulses. Massys, more directly aware of Italianate ideas, produced closely knit forms which enhanced the dramatic quality of the subject. The movement toward these various elements in the works of such artists reflects classical concepts and heralds the advent of the Renaissance spirit in Northern art—most clearly realized in the works of Dürer.

All in all, the Renaissance is one of the most splendid periods in the history of art, and it contains so many great masters that this book can give only brief indications of their work. The most important of the great figures may be said to belong to the following three periods: (1) the Early Renaissance (fifteenth century, *quattrocento*): the budding period; (2) the Late Renaissance (early sixteenth century, *cinquecento*): the fulfillment; and (3) the Northern Renaissance (sixteenth century).

EARLY RENAISSANCE: THE BUDDING PERIOD

The starting point and center of the Early Renaissance was the city of Florence, which produced works of great vision and genius and was to exert a lasting influence on Western art. The development of the arts was stimulated by wealthy citizens, the uncrowned princes of the republic. Among them was the banking family of the Medici, which included the art-loving Cosimo the Elder and his grandson, Lorenzo the Magnificent, a great patron of art and literature.

Giotto can be considered the herald of the Renaissance, but the immediate founder was the Florentine painter *Masaccio* (Tommaso Guidi, 1401–1428) a contemporary of Jan van Eyck. Masaccio's fresco "Expulsion from Eden" (Fig. 13) invites comparison with Van Eyck's "Adam and Eve" (Fig. 5a) on the "Ghent Altarpiece." Both artists painted the human body realistically, but what a difference there is! Van Eyck's figures are portrayed with the precision of an anatomist; Masaccio's, on the other hand, have the illusion of movement—an innovation in painting at this time. Expelled by the angel with a sword, Masaccio's Adam and Eve leave hastily, yet reluctantly, for an unknown future. In contrast to Van Eyck's painting, all details have been left out. The accent is on expression, movement, bodily curves and plasticity, the natural fall of light, and the effects of chiaroscuro. The expressions of contrition and shame, differ-

Fig. 13—MASACCIO: *Expulsion from Eden. Ca.* 1425. The Brancacci Chapel, Santa Maria del Carmine, Florence. (Photo: Alinari)

ent in each of the two figures, are psychologically convincing. Adam's repentance is turned inward; Eve manifests her despair openly. Masaccio's scene is inspired by purely human feeling and is not an expression of medieval symbolism. It is this, then, that differentiates Masaccio from his predecessors and also from his contemporary Fra Angelico.

Fra Angelico (1387–1455), a Dominican friar, conscious of the new achievements of the young Renaissance, remained a medievalist. In his frescoes and paintings in the monastery of San Marco in Florence, he attained a final, beautiful, and pure flowering of medieval devotion.

In contrast to Fra Angelico, the work of his pupil, *Benozzo Gozzoli* (1420–1498), showed the worldly spirit of the Renaissance clearly—as in "Journey of the Magi" (Fig. 14), painted between 1459 and 1463 on the walls of a small chapel in the Palazzo Medici (a building later owned by the Riccardi family and now the Prefecture). Although the subject is the procession of the Three Kings, the religious theme is secondary. Gozzoli, in love with riches and pageantry, has portrayed here a colorful festive occasion of his own day—the visit paid by the Emperor of Constantinople, John Paleologus, to the Council of Florence in the year 1439. The Medicis are depicted as they receive in splendor their illustrious guests, who are accompanied by a large retinue of servants. Among the patricians and artists of the town surrounding these distinguished personages, the artist, who actually saw this visit when he was nineteen years old, has painted himself. Together with the old Cosimo (*Pater Patriae* and head of the family), his sickly son Piero, and other members of the family is his grandson Lorenzo, later called "the Magnificent," who is seen here crowned like a prince in a fairy tale, riding a beautiful white horse and assuming the role of one of the Three Kings. The two outriders have just made a turn and seem to be riding off the wall into the chapel. In the background we see the wide panorama of the Tuscan hills and a long procession of servants, soldiers, and horses all loaded with presents, winding its way over the landscape. In the mountainous countryside with its rocks and trees drawn in the Gothic style, a hunt is taking place. Castles and small towns crown the hills as they still do today. In these frescoes Gozzoli has presented his master work,

Fig. 14.—BENOZZO GOZZOLI: *Journey of the Magi* (detail). *Ca.* 1462. Palazzo Medici. (Photo: Alinari)

Fig. 15—Sandro Botticelli: *Primavera. Ca.* 1478. Uffizi Gallery, Florence. (Photo: Alinari)

a stylish and highly illustrative image of a festivity in the prosperous commercial town of Florence and of the court of its first citizens. The colorful splendor of these chapel walls, however, must have been distracting, rather than inspiring, to devout worshipers.

The true "court" painter of the Medicis was *Sandro Botticelli* (Alessandro Filipepi, 1444?–1510), who lived in the days of Lorenzo. For one of Lorenzo's villas, Botticelli painted his famous "Primavera" (Fig. 15), an allegorical image of spring with mythological figures as large as life painted in delicate hues against a dark background. Flowers, fruit, and the sky between the tree trunks enliven the dark green of the grass and the trees. Spring is the festival of love, and in this symmetrical composition, with figures grouped on both sides, we see Venus in the center; above her flies Cupid, who bends his bow prior to shooting an arrow. Botticelli often turned to pagan sources for his subjects, and in this work the figures of Mary and the Child have been replaced by Venus, who has a natural halo made of leaves, and Cupid. To her right we see Flora, crowned with flowers, scattering blossoms with both hands. Beside her stands a young woman dressed only in a light veil: Primavera, Spring herself, who has been blown into this setting by a young man with bulging cheeks, who symbolizes Zephyr, the wind of spring. To the left of Venus, the artfully interwoven group of the three Graces dances, and to the far left we see Mercury, the messenger of the gods, chasing away the last clouds with his staff.

In this beautiful painting we are impressed more by the rhythm, grace, and melody of line than by the subdued colors in which only the red of Venus' dress stands out. This lyrical painting was an interpretation of an allegorical poem by Angelo Poliziano, the favorite bard of Lorenzo. Botticelli was here dreaming of a flowering magic garden in which fairy-like figures stir rhythmically. With all their grace and beauty, the dreamy figures have an air of melancholy, as do nearly all the figures in Botticelli's paintings, but Primavera herself was intended as a personal, more melancholy remembrance. Lorenzo commissioned this painting to honor the memory of the girl his brother Giuliano loved, Simonetta Vespucci, who died in the spring of 1476 at the age of eighteen. Simonetta served as the model for

Flora in the painting. The aura of sadness around the painting was further intensified, for when the work was finally completed Giuliano himself was no longer alive. In 1478 he was murdered in the choir of the cathedral—a victim of the conspiracy of the Pazzi against the Medici.

Near the end of the fifteenth century the citizens of Florence began to feel uneasy, as if it were the "morning after the feast." Their souls were ready for the sermons of penitence by the Dominican monk Savonarola, who in 1498 was burned at the stake. One of those deeply impressed by Savonarola was Botticelli, whose late works, particularly the Dante drawings, reflect an intensified mysticism.

Many other painters worked in Florence during the *quattrocento*. *Paolo Uccello* (1397–1475), an artist in love with perspective, painted battle scenes and the huge equestrian portrait, "Sir John Hawkwood," in the cathedral of Florence. *Fra Filippo Lippi* (1406–1469) painted worldly Madonnas, and his son, *Filippino Lippi,* another fine artist, worked under the influence of Botticelli. *Domenico Ghirlandajo* (1449–1494) is known especially for his series of frescoes with portraits of the Tornabuoni family in the Santa Maria Novella in Florence, and *Piero di Cosimo* (1462–?1521) was a painter of extraordinary and fertile fantasy.

The brilliance of Florence as a cultural center tends to obscure the contributions made elsewhere. A large number of artists, however, were active outside her domain. In Northern Italy the severe monumentalist *Andrea Mantegna* (1431–1506) painted frescoes in the Eremitani Church in Padua, which is near the Arena Chapel containing the frescoes by Giotto that were largely destroyed in World War II. In Arezzo, the Umbrian *Piero della Francesca* (1416?–?1492) created his frescoes of the "Legend of the True Cross." In these, as in "The Resurrection of Christ" (Fig. 16), may be seen a profound mastery of the technical elements of painting. Piero's work goes further, in that it realizes the cherished ideal of the Renaissance: the perfect balancing of the physical and the spiritual.

In Venice we find *Vittore Carpaccio* (*fl.* 1460–1526) and *Giovanni Bellini* (1428?–1516), the teachers of Giorgione and Titian and the founders of the Venetian School. In Bellini's pictures, particularly, there is a grandeur and monumentality that was

Fig. 16—PIERO DELLA FRANCESCA: *The Resurrection of Christ. Ca.* 1460. Communal Gallery, Borgo San Sepulcro. (Photo: Alinari)

to reach its fullest expression in the Late Renaissance. Two major artists who devoted systematic attention to the problems of anatomical rendering were *Antonio Pollaiuolo* (1432?–?1498) and *Luca Signorelli* (1441–1523). Pollaiuolo's etching of the "Ten Nudes" served as an anatomical source for future artists, among them Dürer. Signorelli painted the side walls of a chapel in the cathedral of Orvieto with his famous fresco of "The Last Judgment," in which the nude found its most grandiose form. His best-known framed painting, the "School of Pan," was painted (according to Vasari) for Lorenzo the Magnificent. Together with 400 other paintings, it was destroyed by fire in May, 1945, only a few days after the Russians occupied Berlin.

LATE RENAISSANCE: THE FULFILLMENT

If the Early Renaissance was a period of search and endeavor and youthful enthusiasm in the discovery of man and nature, we can speak of the years around 1500 as a period of attainment and fulfillment. The artist had by then grasped all the important techniques of painting. He had mastered anatomy, movement, and perspective; he had learned to leave out all superfluous details and to show only the essential ones. Magnificence of form and spiritual content reached a harmonic unity. As we look back on this period through the centuries, it seems as if, after a long ascent, a high plateau was reached, above which, like mountain tops, rose some of the greatest artists the Western world has ever known: Leonardo da Vinci, Michelangelo, Raphael, Giorgione, Titian, and Veronese.

At the beginning of this classic period we find *Leonardo da Vinci* (1452–1519). His great work, "The Last Supper" (Fig. 17), was painted between 1495 and 1498 on a wall of the refectory of Santa Maria delle Grazie in Milan. The subject was a customary one for the dining hall of a monastery. Unfortunately, the work has not been well preserved and has required repeated restoration. It should be judged, therefore, not only from the restored original but also from old copies and engravings. Leonardo's painting is a dramatization of Christ's words, "Verily, verily, I say unto you that one of you shall betray me." The results of more than a century of the study of Man, beginning with Giotto and Masaccio, have been utilized here by one of the great students of the human heart. All the passions and characteristics of spiritually adult human beings are represented in the twelve apostles.

Leonardo's most famous portrait, the "Mona Lisa," also called "La Gioconda," is of Madonna (Mona) Lisa Gherardini, the wife of an important Florentine, Francesco del Giocondo. In this painting Leonardo has depicted his ideal of the mature, noble woman. Unlike many women in the paintings of the *quattro*

Fig. 17—LEONARDO DA VINCI: *The Last Supper. Ca.* 1495–98. Santa Maria delle Grazie, Milan. (Photo: Alinari)

cento, she wears no jewelry. She is a woman with a knowing smile, and her face rises in calm self-assurance above the broad base formed by her crossed arms and beautiful hands. Leonardo has carefully avoided all angularity. The space between her head and shoulders is filled with loosely hanging hair and a veil, so that the face becomes a closed monumental form. Nothing detracts from the life of the soul reflected in the face with its soft smile, the symbol of the "Eternal Woman." Under the diffused light, the shadows are subtle transitions from light to dark, gliding over the face, the dress, and the hands. This is the *sfumato,* about which Leonardo wrote: "A body which is in a moderate light will have but little difference between its lights and shadows; and this comes to pass at the fall of the evening, or when there are clouds: works painted then are soft in feeling and every kind of face acquires a charm." The gay colors in which Gozzoli so delighted have vanished; everything is painted in a golden-brown hue. Behind the parapet we see a lonely mountain landscape, in which a river and a road are lost in the blue distance with its weird peaks—a landscape of the soul.

The same dualism of simplicity of form and spiritual depth is found in the works of the painter and sculptor *Michelangelo Buonarroti* (1475–1564). Twice he accepted papel commissions for frescoes in the Sistine Chapel of the Vatican, named after Pope Sixtus IV, who built it during the latter part of the fifteenth century. For Pope Julius II, Michelangelo decorated the ceiling with illustrations of biblical history from the creation to Noah. Surrounding these scenes are nudes and twelve powerful figures—seven prophets and five prophetesses or sibyls—each seated in a painted niche. Clearly this is the work of a sculptor. The illusion presented is that of a richly detailed architecture and of arches and pillars with gigantic figures; yet, it is achieved entirely through fresco painting. Perhaps this work violates the principle of the pure art of painting, which is bound to the plane and should never try to imitate architecture and sculpture, but this scruple does not diminish the power of Michelangelo's work. "Jeremiah" (Fig. 18), the prophet of doom and singer of plaintive chants, is depicted as the symbol of defeat and melancholy. Although he has a body like a rock, Jeremiah is only an impotent giant. His hand hangs down weakly and his crossed

Fig. 18—MICHELANGELO BUONARROTI: *Jeremiah*. *Ca.* 1508–12. Sistine Chapel, The Vatican, Rome. (Photo: Alinari)

legs are robbed of their strength. Here, no exterior details distract us from the representation of a human being laden with sorrow. The two prophetic figures of sibyls in the background turn away from Jeremiah, thus strengthening the mood of disaster.

Four long years Michelangelo labored under immense strain on the scaffolds to produce the frescoes on the ceiling, unwilling to be helped by others and in constant conflict with the impatient Pope. When, in 1512, the work was finally finished, he

Fig. 19—MICHELANGELO BUONARROTI: *The Last Judgment*. 1536–41. Sistine Chapel, The Vatican, Rome. (Photo: Alinari)

returned to Florence, determined never again to take a brush in hand. Twenty-two years later, however, he began another project in the Sistine Chapel, this time for Pope Paul III. This new commission which occupied him and caused him to suffer for seven years was the great altar wall—"The Last Judgment" (Fig. 19).

Whereas Michelangelo showed passionate emotion in his art, the master from Urbino, *Raphael* (Raffaello Sanzio, 1483–1520),

Fig. 20—RAPHAEL: *Sistine Madonna.* 1528. Museum of Dresden, Dresden.

created works of harmonic beauty, gracious lines, balanced composition, and serenity. Everything in his paintings appears lovely and gentle. Raphael's series of frescoes in the Stanza della Segnatura in the Vatican were painted for Julius II at the time when Michelangelo was working on the ceiling of the Sistine Chapel.

Raphael is known especially as the painter of lovely Madonnas—the "La Belle Jardinière" in the Louvre, the "Tempi Madonna" in Munich, and the "Madonna with the Goldfinch" in Florence. The most famous, the "Sistine Madonna" (Fig. 20), a work which took its name from the church for which it was painted, the San Sisto in Piacenza, has its setting in heaven. The Virgin comes floating down on clouds that in the distance change into heads of innumerable cherubs. Her dress and veil move in the wind. The eyes of Mary and the Child reveal a seriousness and purity not of this earth. The figures on each side of them, citizens of heaven, the patron saints of the church, sink just slightly into the clouds upon which Mary stands weightlessly. On the left is St. Sixtus, a third-century pope (actually a contemporary portrait of the della Rovere pope, Sixtus IV, posing as St. Sixtus). On the right is St. Barbara and behind her can be seen the tower in which she is supposed to have been imprisoned before her martyrdom. Sixtus looks up modestly toward Mary and with a gesture of supplication points in the same direction in which Barbara has turned her downcast eyes. The bottom edge of the painting, on which two little cherubs and the tiara of the pope rest, represents the border between heaven and earth. This edge is actually that of the high altar on which the painting was standing and which Raphael extended into the painting, as he did with the curtains on each side of the altar. The result is that the altar wall appeared to open and to allow the eye to wander in toward the heavenly view. The triangular composition is classic and leads the eye immediately to the center of the painting: the faces of Mary and the Child. Classic too are the nobility of the forms, and the way in which the figures, by their attitudes and gestures, are related to each other as well as to the spectator.

Like Leonardo and Raphael, the Venetian *Giorgione* (Giorgio Barbarelli, 1478?–1510) was looking for perfect beauty. His "Sleeping Venus" (Fig. 21) is perhaps the most beautiful female

Fig. 21—GIORGIONE: *Sleeping Venus*. 1510. Museum of Dresden, Dresden. (Photo: Alinari)

nude in art. Hers is an ideal beauty and perfection; she does not seem to be associated with a model or with any other particular person. The soft flowing lines of her reclining figure are at one with the earth upon which she lies and with the landscape beyond, composed in strong, horizontal lines which surround her with the rest and peace of the evening.

Giorgione was scarcely thirty years old when he died of the plague in Vienna, and the number of his paintings is small. The landscape of his "Sleeping Venus" was inserted after his death by his friend Titian.

One thing distinguishes Giorgione and the other great Venetians, Titian and Veronese, from the Florentines: in Florence, forms were defined by lines; in Venice, by color. Thus, it is understandable why Florence had great sculptors and Venice had none.

Titian (Tiziano Vecelli, 1477?–1576) was the painter of and for the princes of the *cinquecento*. Himself a prince of painters, he dominated the period through his long life and his influence continued long after his death. The rulers of Europe overwhelmed him with tokens of their favor, and Charles V called him his *amico carissimo* ("dearest friend"). A great colorist and a very versatile artist, Titian painted all the subjects of the Renaissance—imposing portraits, voluptuous nudes, and splendid religious and mythological scenes. He passed through a long evolution in which his style became ever more free and finally ended in a rough impressionism. During the course of his evolution, he cast light on all facets of humanity. He showed his sensuousness in his paintings of pagan bacchanalia, but in later life he also painted religious scenes of great dramatic impact.

If we compare Titian's "Entombment" (Fig. 22) with Raphael's "Sistine Madonna," we can distinguish between pictorial and plastic art. Raphael saw his figures as rounded and clearly delineated forms; Titian saw them as areas of color enhanced by contrasts between light and shadow. Raphael concentrated on the lines defining the forms; Titian produced forms whose substance was achieved through color. In the "Entombment," the head and the upper part of the body of Christ are in shadow. This deep shadow, which contrasts with the light of the pale

Fig. 22—TITIAN: *Entombment. Ca.* 1525. Louvre, Paris. (Archives Photographiques, Paris)

flesh and the white sheet, heightens the mystery and the tragedy of death. The composition is simple. In a mighty arc from the lower left corner to the lower right corner, the three bearers of Christ's body—Joseph of Arimathea, John, and Nicodemus—dominate the scene. The body of Christ curves away from them, forming, together with the three bearers, a circle. The two women on the left—Mary, the mother of Jesus, and Mary Magdalene—are balanced by the dark trees to the right. There is no effort to show depth; the figures are all in the same plane and obstruct the view of the horizon.

The sonorous color effects are created by the alternation of light and dark and of warm and cool and by the breaking up of local color into many shades that find their echoes around them. The color scheme runs from the warm red and gold of Nicodemus' cloak on the right, across the pale skin color and the broken white of the sheet, to the cool blue of Mary's robe on the left. This contrast is repeated in the sky where the gold of the sunset fades into the deep blue of the night. Monumental form, rich color, and moving expressions are united in this painting into one whole. The emotion and the strong chiaroscuro point the way toward the approaching Baroque period. Already it is but a short step to Rubens and Rembrandt, both of whom learned much from Titian.

Veronese (Paolo Caliari, 1528–1588), named after his birthplace Verona, became the painter of the gay and festive life of a carefree Venice. It is apparent in his famous banquet scenes that he enjoyed monumental architecture, marble pillars, beautiful women, splendid china, and exquisite food. These festive scenes were often given biblical titles, such as "The Marriage at Cana," and were sometimes painted by Veronese for refectories of monasteries—an indication of a worldly time. In spite of the religious titles, these works are quite thoroughly secular.

Veronese was in the first place a decorative artist and a great colorist, and his works are pageants of color. In contrast to Titian, he preferred silvery hues to golden ones. The transparent atmosphere and the illusion of depth in his paintings are a delight to the eye. As for the composition, it is still based on classic symmetry, but the atmosphere and effect of space point toward the Baroque.

Of the other important *cinquecento* painters we shall mention only a few. In Florence there were the romantic *Andrea del Sarto* and the Dominican *Fra Bartolommeo,* whose portrait of Savonarola can still be seen in the monk's cell in the monastery of San Marco. In Venice we must mention *Palma Vecchio,* the portraitist of blonde Venetian women. In Brescia, *Moroni* became famous for his fine portraits. Finally, in the small town of Parma the painter *Correggio,* using the effects of "magic light" (in his much admired "Holy Night") and a daring perspective and strong movement (in his ceiling of the church of San Giovanni), anticipated the Baroque.

THE NORTHERN RENAISSANCE

The year 1517, the beginning of the Reformation, marked a turning point in Northern painting and a farewell to the Middle Ages. The Reformation shattered the unity and challenged the authority of the Medieval Church, and it prepared the way for a new era. On the one hand, an intensification of religious awareness occurred as new sects arose which paved the way for the Counter Reformation under the leadership of the Society of Jesus (founded in 1534 by Ignatius of Loyola). On the other hand, struggle, independence, and individuality, which resulted in large part from the Reformation, fostered a new spirit of worldliness.

The artist, liberated from the old ecclesiastical traditions, sought freer and more individualistic means of expression. Many sought support and inspiration in Italy, the birthplace of the Renaissance, and the Netherlandish artists who studied and worked in Rome were called "Romanists." The period was one of transition and new masters appeared who reflected this spirit.

Quentin Massys (or Metsys, 1466–1530), a native of Louvain, lived in Antwerp, which in the sixteenth century had assumed the role formerly held by Bruges, the great trading center of Flanders. Although Massys never visited Italy, the influence of Italian artists, especially of Leonardo, is unmistakable in his work. One should think of him, however, not as an imitator but as the great independent artist that he was. He is known especially for his two great triptychs, the St. John and the St. Anna altarpieces, which in composition and architectural structure reflect the characteristics of the Italian Renaissance. Massys also painted secular paintings, such as the "Banker in His Office," the "Money Changer and His Wife," and several beautiful portraits.

In general the great painters who succeeded Massys may be regarded as belonging to the Renaissance. It is these artists who were most profoundly affected by the work of Raphael and Michelangelo. One of the foremost was *Lucas van Leyden* (1494–1533). Although he never visited Italy, he was able to study the works of Raphael through the copper etchings of the Italian artist Marcantonio Raimondi (who later also copied landscape backgrounds from Lucas' pictures). Van Leyden himself achieved fame for his beautiful copper engravings, which were scarcely inferior to those of the master engraver Albrecht Dürer, whom Van Leyden had met once, in 1521, when both were in Antwerp. Except for brief absences on a few trips to this city, he remained in the town of his birth until his death.

Van Leyden's work was new in two respects: his style was looser and more fluent than that of other fifteenth-century painters and his subjects were different. Besides religious subjects, he painted scenes depicting the everyday activities of peasants and citizens, such as a girl milking a cow or men pulling their carts.

Van Leyden's paintings are rare today, but his masterpiece, "The Last Judgment" (Fig. 23), survived the religious wars. This work has the traditional form of a triptych, although the wings no longer frame the middle panel with solemn saints. The three parts form one continuous composition. The movement radiates outward from the center, continues to the left and the right on the side panels, and seems to continue even beyond the frame. Along with the gay quality of the painting, this almost whimsical cutting-off of the figures adds to an impression of enormous space, even of infinity. This work shows how far Van Leyden had moved away from the stately, motionless, confined style of the fifteenth-century masters. Also, in depicting the free movement and the anatomy of the nudes he attained results which no Northern painter had yet achieved. The outstanding feature of his painting, however, is the light that seems to radiate from it and to dominate all the other paintings in the room where it is exhibited. (One wonders whether even the nineteenth-century Impressionists, light-painters par excellence, would have been

Fig. 23.—LUCAS VAN LEYDEN: *The Last Judgment*. *Ca.* 1526. Museum "de Lakenhal," Leiden.

able to improve upon this masterful work.) The paint has been applied thinly and transparently, and the sketch underneath on the panels shows through clearly. On the back of the side panels are the figures of Peter (the patron saint of Leiden) and of Paul. Both are life-sized and display strong emotions. They are seated on rocks, and in the background are mountains and tiny islands. For sheer glory of painting, Van Leyden's figures are as outstanding as those painted by Dürer in the same year, 1526.

An early landscape painter was *Joachim Patinir* (1485?–1524), a native of Dinant, who did most of his work in Antwerp. His paintings contain tiny incidental figures providing titles for the pictures, such as the "Flight to Egypt." What he really intended to emphasize was the landscapes, only a few of which, however, he painted "pure," that is, without the tiny figures. His wide panoramas, the high horizons, and the freakish rock formations remind one of the region where Patinir was born, along the rocky shores of the Meuse River.

Jan Mostaert (1475?–1555) devoted his attention almost exclusively to religious subjects; yet, surprisingly, he painted, around 1520, a West Indian landscape in which Spanish soldiers are shown fighting the Indians. This appears to be based on reports then reaching Europe about the discoveries of the Spaniards in the West Indies.

The trend away from traditional religious subjects, introducing a new emphasis on contemporary people and their environment, found its most effective expression in the work of *Pieter Bruegel the Elder* (1529?–1569). A native of Brabant (he was born in the village of Bruegel, near Breda), he worked for several years in Antwerp and eventually settled in Brussels, which was then the capital of Brabant. He did not associate himself with international Mannerism but instead continued the Netherlands tradition, thus paving the way for the Dutch masters of the seventeenth century.

Bruegel made the customary pilgrimage to Italy, but he refused to imitate the figures in Raphael's frescoes in the Stanza or the nudes in Michelangelo's "Last Judgment." He returned, instead, with drawings of the Alpine world. Karel van Mander once said that Bruegel painted as if he had "swallowed all those mountains and rocks, to disgorge them at home on canvas and panels." On

Fig. 24—Pieter Bruegel the Elder: *Fall of Icarus. Ca.* 1558. Musée des Beaux-Arts, Brussels.

Fig. 25—Pieter Bruegel the Elder: *Census in Bethlehem,* 1556. Musée des Beaux-Arts. Brussels.

his Italian journey Bruegel traveled all the way to the Strait of Messina which he painted as the scene of the "Fall of Icarus" (Fig. 24). This painting, his sole effort to deal with a mythological subject, depicts Icarus (who had attempted to fly toward the sun) plunging into the sea. But it is quite difficult to identify the subject, for all one sees of Icarus is a pair of kicking legs vanishing in the water. A majestic ship is proceeding under full sail, but nobody on it pays any attention to Icarus. Neither the fisherman nor the shepherd in the scene look in his direction. The largest figure, a peasant in the foreground, continues his plowing, completely unaware of Icarus' hazardous enterprise and its tragic ending. The distaste for hero worship here displayed is characteristic alike of Bruegel and of the Netherlands as a whole. Even the most daring hero becomes insignificant when contrasted with the powers of nature. Against the background of this heroic event, Bruegel sees the common man as the only constant element in the world.

Bruegel did not glorify individuals in his paintings as the painters of the Italian Renaissance had done through their emphasis on the great leaders, the merchant princes, and the *condottiere*. Renaissance sculptors were commissioned to commemorate such men. With Bruegel the individual disappeared into the mass. Unlike his predecessors Bruegel was not the servant of the Church. From his lookout on high he surveyed the human anthill on which there is no room for saints or heroes but only for the common people. Here every man plays his role and is moved by the same passions.

The setting for the "Census in Bethlehem" (Fig. 25) is a Brabant village in a winter landscape. In this painting the short December day comes to its end and the sun sets blood-red behind a bare tree. Between the houses and across the frozen river, people are shown moving about in busy activity. In the foreground a pig is being slaughtered. The townspeople are carrying wood and the children are playing their age-old games: they throw snowballs, spin tops, and coast downhill on sleds. On the riverbank one youngster is putting on his skates. In the left foreground, in an inn with a green wreath hanging over its door, the officials of the Emperor Augustus have seated themselves with their books, and here the people dutifully gather to register.

Almost unnoticed, Joseph is making his way between the wagons with his ox and the ass on which Mary is seated. These figures have become merely two human beings among others. The whole scene, however, would be confusing and crowded if it were not for the gentle snow with its white expanse framing the restless movements of the people and giving them unity.

Other works of Bruegel, too, reflect his tendency to use his immediate surroundings and everyday life as the settings for great historical dramas, which clearly allude to events of his own time. The setting of "The Massacre of the Innocents" is a snowy village. Herod's butchering soldiers wear the red coats of the infamous mercenaries of Spain. The association is clear: this painting was completed in 1567, on the eve of the War against Spain, when mercenaries in the service of Spain were carrying out bloody raids on defenseless towns and villages in the Netherlands.

Those were cruel days and Bruegel, too, could give expression to cruel sentiments. He should not be regarded as the gay painter of peasant life, as so many have judged him since the time of Karel van Mander. With all his sympathy for humanity, Bruegel was a pessimist; behind the human scene, the sinister figure of death grins constantly. His extraordinary painting of the "Triumph of Death" and his grim painting of "The Blind Leading the Blind" both illustrate his pessimism.

Bruegel landscapes depicting the months of the year—such as the beautiful winter landscape "Hunters in the Snow"—surpass in vision and composition any other such work of the sixteenth century, including those by his sons Pieter and Jan. Not until the Dutch landscape artists of the seventeenth century were there any worthy successors to him in this art form.

We have no portraits by Bruegel (with the exception of a single self-portrait sketch), probably because humanity as a whole interested him much more than individual personalities. *Anton Mor* (1519–1575), on the other hand, was an expert portraitist and the finest Netherlandish portrait painter before Rembrandt, Frans Hals, and Van Dyck. A native of Utrecht, he became a figure of international renown, working as a court painter for Philip II in Madrid. Mor belonged to the realistic Netherlands school, but he studied Titian's art and this helped him give his portraits an imposing and alluring air. Soberly and in a business-like fashion but with sharp psychological insight, he painted the grandees of his days: Philip II, Mary Tudor, the Duke of Alba, Margaret of Parma. He also painted Prince William of Orange as a youth, a portrait now in the Museum of Kassel.

In those unsettled years after 1500, when art turned from the Gothic to the Renaissance style tempered by the spirit of the Reformation, German painting achieved its fullest flowering, even surpassing for a time the art of the Netherlands. Instead of being further influenced by them, the German artists, particularly the painter Albrecht Dürer, effected a profound influence upon the artists of the Netherlands.

The greatest masterpiece of German art during this period, the "Isenheim Altar," was created by a painter who worked in obscurity and without any outside influence. The extraordinary art creations of this man, *Matthias Grünewald* (only recently has research disclosed his real name, Mathis Nithart, 1460?–?1528), must be included among the outstanding achievements of Western art. His work reached expressive heights and has stirred the human spirit from his day to the present. (In 1938 Paul Hindemith composed the opera *Mathis der Maler* about him). Grünewald belonged to the school of artists frequently encountered in the northern countries who, in those days of realism, rose above realistic reproduction and moved in an atmosphere of fantasy and dream. These artists painted not visual reality but vision, not the outer but the inner world. In the Netherlands such men were Hieronymus Bosch, Rembrandt, Hercules Seghers, and more recently Vincent van Gogh. In France, where a taste for moderation and clarity in art predominates, there are none—with the possible exception of Odilon Redon. In Spain, the visionary artists include El Greco (like Grünewald, a mystic) and Goya.

The "Isenheim Altar" was painted for the monastery of St. Anthony of Isenheim, situated against a slope of the Vosges mountains in northern Alsace. Like many other German altarpieces, this work is a combination of painted panels and sculpture. According to the needs of the church festivals, it could be opened and closed in various ways, and one could "leaf in it as in a book." At present the panels of this altarpiece are exhibited separately. When the work is closed, it shows the Crucifixion

Fig. 26—MATTHIAS GRÜNEWALD: *Concert of Angels before the Madonna* from the *Isenheim Altar,* 1509–1511. Musée d'Unterlinden, Colmar.

in the center—a ghastly scene of sombre color against a background of night and desolation. Painted in a grayish-green color, the body of Christ is covered with wounds and portrays terrible suffering and death. The fingers are lifted toward the sky. The head has sunk on the chest and the feet are torn and swollen. Never has a martyr's death in all its horror been painted more fiercely and more shockingly. Below the cross we find the traditional figures of Mary, John, and Magdalene. There is also another figure—John the Baptist, who points to Christ uttering the words from the Gospel of John, "He must increase, but I must decrease."

On the inner panels—the "Annunciation," the "Concert of Angels before the Madonna" (Fig. 26), and the "Resurrection of Christ"—this sombreness gives way to gaiety, and the mystery of the Incarnation and the Resurrection is revealed. In the "Concert of Angels before the Madonna," we see choirs of angels underneath the baldachin. The background recedes into blue and gray, and in the foreground an angel plays the viola da gamba. Mary rests in a garden surrounded by roses and a little wall, the *hortus conclusus* ("enclosed garden"), a symbol of purity. The Child in the torn diapers, the little bed and the bath, and the happiness of the Mother are all of this world and portray Christ as a human child. The background again is a vision: above the blue mountains and the color-play of the clouds the skies open and God the Father is seen among rows of angels who announce the birth to shepherds barely visible in the radiant light.

With Grünewald color has been used to convey a new meaning: it has become a means of interpreting various emotions—despair and joy, sorrow and happiness. Not until Vincent van Gogh would color again be handled so effectively as a means of expressing emotion.

Whereas little is known about the life of Grünewald, *Albrecht Dürer* (1471–1528), master of Nuremberg, was famous during his lifetime for his woodcuts and engravings as well as his paintings. He sprang from the traditions of the late Gothic but rose above the ingenuousness of the Middle Ages to become the self-assured Renaissance man, the most versatile painter and creative genius in the history of German art. Very much a child of the spiritual life of his time and country—the Germany of Martin Luther—he journeyed to Italy twice, in 1495 and 1506, to learn more about perspective, anatomy, and proportion. And later, in 1512, when he was temporarily without inspiration and in need of new impressions, he visited the Netherlands and met the contemporary masters Quentin Massys and Lucas van Leyden in Antwerp.

Dürer constantly studied nature on all levels, as evidenced by the beautiful water colors of a columbine, a squirrel, and a crab. He began painting landscapes around 1500, not merely as backgrounds for holy scenes but as subjects in themselves. All Dürer's work suggests inner tension, reflecting his wholehearted interest in the moral significance of art.

Toward the end of his life, he painted the famous "Four Apostles" (Fig. 27) and presented it as a gift to be hung in the town hall of Nuremberg. The way the large folds of the garments flow (not angularly and sharply broken as in the Gothic style)

Fig. 27—ALBRECHT DÜRER: *Four Apostles*. 1523–26. Alte Pinakothek, Munich.

evidence Dürer's familiarity with the Italian Renaissance; the lines of the folds lead rapidly to the heads, in which all the expression is concentrated. Like Leonardo in his "Last Supper," Dürer has presented different characteristics of man in the four temperaments of his apostles. John is melancholy; Peter, phlegmatic; Paul (actually not an apostle), sanguinary and nervous; and Mark, choleric. The two figures in the foreground are painted in simple, strong colors: Paul wears a white coat which has bluish shadows, and John wears red over a green undergarment. The double panel was painted in the year 1526 at a time when Nuremberg was the scene of religious strife. With these four imposing figures Dürer wanted to show the townspeople what kind of men, in spite of differences in temperament, true Christians should be. Thus, these two panels serve both as an exhortation and as a declaration of faith.

Lucas Cranach the Elder (1472–1553) belonged to the circle of Martin Luther (whose portrait he painted) and was court painter to Frederick the Wise, Elector of Saxony in Wittenberg. One of his early and most attractive works is the "Rest on the Flight" with a romantic German mountain landscape in the background. Its freshness and poetic inspiration cannot be found among later paintings, most of which were portraits issuing in rapid succession from his large studio.

Wolf Huber and *Albrecht Altdorfer* from the Danube region were best-known as painters of landscapes—an art form which became popular shortly after 1500. Huber also produced pen-and-ink sketches of trees and sunrises. (Leonardo da Vinci had made the first pen-and-ink drawing of a natural scene in 1473.) Jakob Burckhardt, the Swiss historian, has called the discovery of the beauty of the landscape one of the most important events of the new era. Although such painters as Dirk Bouts, Geertgen tot Sint Jans, and Gerard David had taken the first steps in the field, South German masters of the School of the Danube made important contributions to its development.

Both Germany and the Netherlands were on their way toward a flowering of the art of landscape painting. In Germany, however, the evolution did not proceed beyond the brief period of Dürer's water colors and the School of the Danube, whereas in the Netherlands it continued logically with the great landscapes of Bruegel and reached its summit in the seventeenth century with Rubens, Rembrandt, Hercules Seghers, Van Goyen, and Ruisdael.

The portrait also played a large role in early sixteenth-century German painting, as a result of the new self-assurance and prosperity of the citizens. One of the greatest of all portrait painters was *Hans Holbein* (1497?–1543), called "the Younger" to distin-

Fig. 28—HANS HOLBEIN: *Sir Thomas More*. 1527. Frick Collection, New York. (Copyright The Frick Collection, New York)

guish him from his father, also a great master. Born in Augsburg, Holbein spent his early life in Basle. Later, he moved to London where English nobility offered him a more profitable existence than did the small merchants of Basle. In England, Holbein painted Henry VIII and his many wives, Sir Thomas More, Thomas Cromwell, ladies of the court, ambassadors, and dignitaries. One of his first outstanding masterpieces of this period is the portrait of "Sir Thomas More" (Fig. 28). With extraordinary insight Holbein has penetrated the character of the undaunted chancellor of Henry VIII. Thomas More, great humanist and author of *Utopia,* was a close friend of Erasmus, whose portrait Holbein also painted.

Whereas Dürer grew up during the Gothic period and had to learn to master the large forms of the Renaissance, Holbein was born in the Renaissance and his work evidences the tranquility and harmonic and classic structure of the art of the time. His work is a product of cool objectivity. With painters like Dürer and Rembrandt, one senses immediately that the artist sympathized with his models and that he did not hide his feelings toward his subjects. Holbein, on the other hand, remained objective and unmoved. Depicting his subjects with an astonishingly sharp eye and combining the impartiality of the camera with the selectivity and synthesis of form which a photograph can never give, he became the ideal portrait painter. Most of these expressive portraits, though small, are unsurpassed in precise observation and fine execution. His precision was such that he could also produce fine miniatures; some beautiful ones are no larger than a hand.

Holbein was the last important master during this period of the flowering of German art. Not until the nineteenth century would any German painters of consequence again emerge.

10

Mannerism

(ca. *1525–1600*)

In the art of Michelangelo the Renaissance reached its summit and Mannerism found its starting point. Michelangelo was the artist whom all others admired. To surpass him was inconceivable; it seemed that art could have only one purpose: to follow his way (*maniera*) of painting. Thus, the development of art was carried forward into the transition period known as Mannerism.

Three magnificent frescoes marked the development of Michelangelo as a painter: the first was a battle scene (1504)—since lost and replaced by a painting by Vasari—in the great town hall of the Palazzo Vecchio in Florence; the second was the ceiling of the Sistine Chapel (1508–1512); the third was the colossal "Last Judgment" (1536–1541) high above the altar of the same chapel. In these compositions Michelangelo portrayed the naked human body in the most complicated postures, movements, and perspectives, and with a daring and a plasticity which astounded his contemporaries. What Italy had been seeking for more than a century had been achieved with unbelievable perfection in these almost superhuman figures full of inner vitality and expressive power.

Artists came to Rome from all over Europe to study these figures and to copy them. While other great masters of the Renaissance—Leonardo da Vinci, Raphael, and Titian—each had in his own way attained what at the time seemed to be the ultimate in the art of painting, Michelangelo stood above the rest. Mannerist artists, inspired by the High Renaissance creations, worked out a style in which the qualities of refinement and elegance were pursued. The classic, symmetrical composition of the Renaissance gave way to an asymmetrical one and became a graceful weaving play of lines. Figures lost their natural proportions, serenity, and equilibrium; body forms became elongated; and nudes posed in sinuous, elegant, and completely unnatural attitudes.

In turning from natural forms and realism, Mannerism bears some relation to modern art. The distortion of the figures painted by the Mannerists Parmigianino and Bronzino can be found again in a twentieth-century Modigliani. This relationship, possibly connected with the uncertainty about life in both the Mannerist and modern periods, has resulted in renewed appreciation of Mannerist art.

The Renaissance remained Italian in its origins and fulfillment; Mannerism, however, was international. Italian artists, invited by King Francis I to work on decorations for the palace at Fontainebleau, carried the new style to France, and artists of England, the Netherlands, Germany, and Spain soon reflected the Mannerist spirit. But the most famoust Mannerist painters came from the South. Although the list of artists is a long one, we shall mention two who may be regarded as most important.

Tintoretto (Jacopo Robusti, 1518–1594) took his name from his father's profession and was called the "little dyer" (*Il Tintoretto*). The last in a series of great Venetian masters, he was a contemporary of Veronese and nowadays is considered the greater painter. The art of Veronese displays carefree gaiety; that of Tintoretto, on the other hand, has an intensely religious and dramatic character and it is no wonder that he was much impressed by Michelangelo's "Last Judgment." Above the door of his studio, he even inscribed "Il desegno di Michelangelo, il colorito di Tiziano" ("The drawing of Michelangelo, the color of Titian"). He was a very prolific genius, who painted enormous canvases rapidly and with unbelievable ease. Anyone who has visited the palace of the Doge knows his decorative wall paintings and ceilings. In the great council room is his "Paradise," one of the largest oil paintings in the world—more than seventy feet wide and twenty-three feet high. The Scuola di San Rocco in Venice (next to the Frari where Titian's works can be admired)

Fig. 29—TINTORETTO: *The Last Supper*. *Ca.* 1592–94. San Giorgio, Venice. (Photo: Alinari)

is a true Tintoretto museum. Between 1560 and 1588 Tintoretto decorated the rooms with fifty-six huge canvases, which have darkened considerably in the course of time. In spite of the gigantic commission, he found time to paint hundreds of other paintings, many of large dimensions.

Whereas the Renaissance accented the individual, Tintoretto preferred the dramatic expressiveness of large crowds. With Tintoretto, scenes full of light and energy, large gestures, and the flickering play of light and dark—elements which bind his compositions into a dynamic unity—have replaced the static, symmetrical compositions of Bellini, Giorgione, and Raphael.

"The Last Supper" (Fig. 29), painted around 1590 toward the end of Tintoretto's life, stands in strong contrast to the symmetry used by Leonardo for the same subject earlier. Here we find ourselves not in a richly decorated Renaissance palace (which would be the setting given such a scene by Veronese) but in more modest and less clearly defined surroundings. The diagonal of the long table quickly leads into depth; the apostles seated on the far side and at each end of the table are simple men, united in a solemn meeting. Gone is the classic harmony and the uniform lighting. Tintoretto has infused the scene with a new drama, an emotional intensity. One would expect to find Christ in the center foreground; instead, he has been put in the background, while in the foreground are large figures of servants. A current of movement runs from the figures on the right, through the waitresses and seated apostles in the center, and finally sweeps into depth to concentrate on the central figure. Counterdiagonals and spirals balance the thrust and carry the eye to Christ, who is breaking bread for the busily gesticulating apostles.

The gestures and poses of the figures heighten the drama. Foreground figures are caught in strong *contrapposto* positions—a typical Mannerist treatment in which equilibrium is achieved by mutually opposite movements of parts of the body. (The term *figura serpentina* is sometimes applied to such figures.) The gestures are broad and theatrical; the light unifies the composition and intensifies the theme. Strong chiaroscuro blurs the contours of the figures and dissolves them into space, whereas intense light surrounds the figure of Christ and reflects on those around him. A smoking oil lamp casts a whimsical flickering light and pellucid angels circle in its haze.

The genre quality of the foreground figures and their activities contrasts strongly with the mystical nature of the background. The two are linked by the light, composition, and theme, and the "realism" of both is thereby heightened.

In spite of the "everyday" character of the foreground, the religious inspiration of a work of this kind is strongly felt. With Veronese this is hardly the case. Veronese was once questioned by the Inquisition because of the worldly spirit of his biblical meals. Tintoretto, however, was an ardent believer, who placed his art in the service of the Catholic Church. In "The Last Supper" he has evoked a magical atmosphere which makes him akin to the Protestant painter, Rembrandt.

To many people, the greatest Mannerist painter is *El Greco* (Domeniko Theotokopoulos, 1541–1614). Born in Crete, he later studied in Italy, probably in the studio of Tintoretto in Venice, and here may have adopted the unusual compositions and the elongated figures of the Mannerist style. In 1577 he went to live in the fortress town of Toledo on the banks of the river Tagus in Spain, and here he developed a style so personal and so possessed by an inner vision that he remained without followers in Spain and was hardly known abroad. Rubens made a diplomatic mission to Spain in the year 1603, after which he wrote that he had not found a single painter worth mentioning. And yet El Greco was highly esteemed in Toledo. He was overwhelmed with commissions for religious paintings and portraits and lived in grand style. After his death he was quickly forgotten, only to be rediscovered around 1900 as the spiritual father of Expressionism, which departed from natural forms and colors and strove for greater force of expression, assigning greater value to the spiritual content of the subject than to realistic delineation.

One of El Greco's most important and largest works is the "Burial of Count Orgaz" (Fig. 30), painted for the funeral chapel of the Orgaz family in the San Tomé in Toledo. It depicts a local legend, a miracle which took place long ago. According to the legend, the count, a pious knight who had founded the church, died and St. Stephen and St. Augustine descended from heaven and carefully carried his body to his grave. In the painting, the two saints lift up the count, who is resplendent in armor and who appears to be sleeping rather than dead. This miracle takes place

Fig. 30—El Greco: *Burial of Count Orgaz.* 1586. San Tomé, Toledo, Spain. (Photo: MAS)

in the foreground; the painter placed a group of his own contemporaries from Toledo in the background. El Greco himself is the sixth figure from the left in the row above the head of St. Stephen, and the boy kneeling at the left is his son, Jorge Manuel. The row of spectators would remind us of a Dutch group portrait if it were not that the minds of these solemn men are directed away from the earth and concentrated on the heavens.

Already the priest and a few others cast their eyes skyward, toward the opening in the blanket of clouds which reveals heaven with its angels and saints. One angel with widespread wings carries the soul of the deceased—a ray of light in human shape—through the clouds toward Mary and John the Baptist and further on to Christ, on his throne high above them. Behind Mary we recognize Peter with his keys, and behind John the Baptist is Paul.

All the figures are portrayed with realistic clarity; nevertheless, we are caught up in a world of dream and vision. Any indication of local situation or depth is lacking; the ground and even the feet of the people are invisible, and the figures themselves seem to be deprived of all earthly weight. The licking flames of the torches, like the thin figures with the small heads, all point to the skies, where the composition of zigzag diagonals is free of movement—in strong contrast to the static group on earth. With El Greco, the vision was a mystical one, directed toward heaven, the goal of all human endeavor.

Like Tintoretto, El Greco was already standing with one foot in the early Baroque, the art of the Counter Reformation. The fanaticism and mysticism of Spanish Catholicism, the spirit of the Jesuits and the Inquisition, still live in his work; yet it lacks the worldly realism of the Baroque, the realistic portrayal of heavenly things. With El Greco the soul striving ever upward reminds us of the spirit of Gothic and even of Byzantine art—but only in spirit. Composition and technique are completely new. The undulating rhythm in the painting is magnificent and the brush strokes are free and impressionistic. A religious enthusiast like Grünewald, he increasingly portrayed his figures in unearthly, elongated forms. El Greco also painted portraits of severe inquisitors from Toledo—noblemen and priests with fanatical faces. Only rarely did he turn to the mythology of antiquity so beloved by the Renaissance and the Baroque.

El Greco's color, especially in his later work, is often a leaden gray-blue with lemon-yellow and sky-blue spots—icy colors which cloak the spiritual fire. Although these cool colors remind us of those used by Vermeer, El Greco, the exalted visionary, is far removed from the quiet Vermeer of Delft.

Twice El Greco painted the town of Toledo itself, and he also used it as background for a number of paintings (once to replace the city of Troy for the "Laocoön," now in the National Gallery, Washington, D.C.). His well-known "View of Toledo" (in the Metropolitan Museum of Art in New York) is not a view of everyday reality but a vision of the town as it is momentarily lit up during the night under blue-black storm clouds. On the steep hills high above the Tagus River flowing through the valley below, we see Toledo with its wall, cathedral, and Alcazar—an unreal vision, dreamlike even in its color. The dull greens and browns are mysteriously charged by a silver-gray moonlight that plays on houses and towers. How different this painting is from Vermeer's "View of Delft" with its radiant, daylight colors! The difference is not so much in the towns themselves as in the personalities of the artists.

In general, paintings of the sixteenth century are difficult to classify. Remnants of the Gothic and Renaissance styles are found alongside the Mannerist style. Although Mannerism was dominant and produced a few great artists, this period should be considered one of crisis in art. In spite of the high quality of its paintings, Mannerism was actually a time of transition—in Italy, between the Renaissance and the Baroque; in the Netherlands, between late Gothicism and the Baroque.

11

Baroque Art

(1575–1700)

The word "Baroque" is generally used when speaking of the art of the seventeenth and the first half of the eighteenth centuries. It was probably derived from the Portuguese *barroco,* the name of an irregularly shaped pearl often worn as fanciful jewelry in the sixteenth and seventeenth centuries. The term is frequently used disparagingly to mean heavy, pompous, and extravagant. As applied to art, however, "Baroque" is understandable if we consider it a description of historical forces at work in a certain period.

Baroque art was closely connected with the struggle for religious power and the new flowering of Catholicism after its low ebb during the Renaissance and Reformation. In the Renaissance, the people were still essentially religious, despite a reverence for the thinkers and poets of antiquity. Then in the North, the Reformation began to make progress, and in the South, Rome tried to reconquer lost ground with the Counter Reformation—if need be, with violence. The Society of Jesus was an effective instrument of the Counter Reformation. Science and art were fettered and "heathenish" subjects banned. Finally, in the early seventeenth century, Europe was divided into two camps—Protestant in the North and Catholic in the South.

In the Northern Netherlands, realistic art—Calvinistic, austere, and intended for the houses of citizens and for council chambers—developed. The Counter Reformation, on the other hand, striving to expand politically, used art for the purpose of extolling saints and martyrs and for lauding the glory and triumph of the Church. The Counter Reformation, which went hand in hand with the absolutism of the princes, made its demands on art and required paintings of battles, historical scenes, and allegorical images for the greater glory of the princes and the nobility. Thus, the Baroque had its heyday in Catholic countries under absolute rule—Italy, the Southern Netherlands, Spain, and Francc.

The Baroque style displayed a new spirit. It was not directed, as the Mannerist and the Renaissance styles were, toward pleasing intellectuals and connoisseurs, but rather toward influencing the masses; to that end it used effective means: dramatic scenes with movement and large gestures, strong contrasts of light and dark, and realistic scenes from the life of the people. In the work of Rubens, the most typical Baroque painter, we find a sensuous ness and an earthy love of life revealed. The harmonic balance of the Renaissance has been replaced by a broader style in which the large lines and figures become more important than the details and in which forms are presented no longer by line but by strong color and value contrasts. In other words the linear and sculptural forms have given way to coloristic and painterly ones.

The Italian Renaissance was born from a scientific and reflective attitude; the Baroque issued from an intuitive and explosive spirit. The static equilibrium, the containment, and the tranquillity of the Italian Renaissance were transformed into the dynamic movement, emotion, and unrest of the Baroque. The Renaissance sought unity through the balance and clarity of separate forms—by *co-ordination*. In the Baroque, unity was achieved through tension and the interrelations of large forms or masses—by *subordination*.

ITALY

Elements of Italian Baroque art had already appeared in the Mannerism of Michelangelo ("Last Judgment"), Titian, and Tintoretto. The creator of the realistic or naturalistic trend in the Baroque, however, was *Caravaggio* (1573–1610). He chose his models from among the common people, whether for genre or for religious paintings. The models for his cardsharps, soothsayers,

Fig. 31—CARAVAGGIO: *Death of the Virgin. Ca.* 1605. Louvre, Paris. (Archives Photographiques, Paris)

and saints were brought into his atelier from the streets of Rome. "Our days," he said, "offer many models, beautiful or ugly. Why must one seek them in antiquity?" Once, a religious painting was refused by the church which had commissioned it because it showed Matthew as a farmer with dirty feet.

His "Death of the Virgin" (Fig. 31) shows the bedside of a woman of the people, and the atmosphere reminds one of the phrase, "Dust thou art and unto dust shalt thou return." Still, this painting is not profane or irreligious. The apostles are common people, but their faces have been ennobled by the sorrow which they share at the passing of the mother of their beloved Master. The painting, however, was considered irreverent and was removed from the church for which it was painted. With his revolutionary realism, Caravaggio was in conscious opposition to Renaissance ideals of beauty.

In his paintings Caravaggio used an artificial, strongly concentrated lighting, which showed certain parts intensely and left others enveloped in shadows. This use of light served to heighten the realism and intensify the drama of his works. Caravaggio's chiaroscuro found its followers all over Europe and influenced many artists, especially in Spain and the Netherlands.

SOUTHERN NETHERLANDS

Although Baroque art was of Italian origin, its greatest master was not an Italian but a Fleming: *Peter Paul Rubens* (1577–1640). The "Romanists" of the sixteenth century had tried unsuccessfully to master the grand style of the Italians. With Rubens this dream became a reality: his strong genius would not imitate a foreign style but would learn instead to transcend it. In his work Italian idealism, form and composition, and the flowering color of the Venetians were joined to Flemish power, realism, and sensuousness. A painter of enormous versatility, possessing an inexhaustible imagination, he mastered all subjects. With astounding ease there flowed from his brush whole series of religious, mythological, and allegorical compositions, as well as impressive landscapes and portraits full of vitality.

Like Titian, Rubens was a "prince of painters" and a painter of royalty. He ruled the art of his time and his country, had a high place in society, undertook diplomatic missions, and was a familiar figure in the courts of Europe. Born in Siegen in Westphalia and raised in Antwerp, he began his real schooling in 1600 when he went to Italy to live. Eight years later, an accomplished master, he returned to Antwerp and became the court painter of the Archduke and Archduchess, Albert and Isabella, in Brussels. His fame spread quickly all over Europe.

One of his first large commissions in Antwerp was the great altarpiece, "The Raising of the Cross" (Fig. 32), painted for the church of St. Walburga (since destroyed), and now in the cathedral of Antwerp along with two other well-known works, "The Descent from the Cross" and "The Assumption of Mary." The painting still has the traditional form of the triptych (our illustration shows only the middle panel); however, the three-panel division is only for the sake of appearances, as it was a hundred years earlier in Lucas van Leyden's "Last Judgment." The theme of "The Raising of the Cross" is typically Baroque. (In earlier days the Crucifixion itself would have been painted.) The choice of subject reflects the Baroque preference for strong movement, muscular bodies, action, and turbulence. The painting, composed along the diagonal, shows a group of Herculean men lifting the heavy cross with almost superhuman effort. Enormous energy emanates from this tumultuous scene and extends to the side panels: on the left, a group of mourning women retreats; on the right, a Roman captain reins in his horse with a sudden pull. Christ is no longer depicted as an emaciated Gothic ascetic, but as a strong, athletic figure entirely of this world—an ideal form which Rubens created. There is no tragedy in the scene. This painting, with its glorification of the power of healthy bodies, is like a paean to life's victory over death; at the same time it is a symbol of the Church triumphant.

In addition to the great altarpieces, Rubens often portrayed mythological and allegorical subjects. The allegory, a favorite subject of the Renaissance and Baroque, can be better understood if we know that the personages presented in the form of gods and goddesses, knights in mail, or beautiful young women represent specific concepts, such as virtues or vices.

Rubens painted whole series of these allegories. One of the best known is his cycle of canvases which Marie de Médicis, widow

Fig. 32—PETER PAUL RUBENS: *The Raising of the Cross.* 1610–11. Antwerp Cathedral, Antwerp. (Copyright A.C.L. Brussels)

of Henry IV of France, commissioned in order to glorify her and her husband's rule. All the Olympian gods and goddesses are represented as protectors and admirers constantly intervening in the life of the queen. These are magnificent paintings (especially in the first designs), but historical fabrications. It has been said that the classic painter Ingres, to shield himself from such extravaganzas, opened his umbrella when he passed this series in the Louvre. One of Rubens' most beautiful allegories is his "Allegory of War" in the Pitti Palace in Florence. Painted toward the end of his life, when all of Europe was at war, this work was highly to the point. Jakob Burckhardt, the historian, has called it "an eternal and unforgettable frontispiece for the Thirty Years' War." As an illustration of the art of the Baroque—with the fierce passions and the violence of unbridled movement which flow through the paintings in large diagonals, it remains unexcelled. Rubens himself explained his work in a letter. In order to show what can be contained in an allegory, we shall present here his description:

> The main figure is Mars, who with shield and bloody sword storms out of the opened Janus temple (which according to Roman usage was closed in times of peace and open in times of war) threatening the people with great disasters. In vain his mistress Venus, surrounded by cupids, tries to hold him back. The fury Alecto, holding a burning torch, pulls him on. The monsters in the upper right symbolize plague and starvation, the faithful companions of war. On the ground lies a woman with a broken lute, indicating that harmony cannot exist simultaneously along with the confusion of war. A mother with a child in her arms is evidence that fertility and love of one's fellow man are destroyed by the disastrous war. An architect has been thrown on his back still clutching his compass, and that represents the idea that what is built in times of peace is destroyed by force of arms. If I remember rightly, a book and some drawings under the feet of Mars indicate that war treads on poetry and the beautiful arts. The mourning woman dressed in black with a torn veil, stripped of all her ornaments, is unhappy Europe, already suffering many years from the plundering, destructions, and misery of the war. Her attribute, carried by an angel, is the globe with a cross on top of it, signifying the Christian World.

Rubens left an enormous heritage of more than two thousand paintings. All were not, however, entirely his own work. In his huge workshop, which was almost a painting factory, numerous helpers assisted. For the great decorative works of his later years, Rubens usually made only a small oil sketch. These are very spontaneous and free and belong to his best work. The museums of Brussels and Rotterdam have many of them; in Rotterdam one can find the beautiful series "Life of Achilles," intended to be executed in tapestry.

All seventeenth-century painters of the Southern Netherlands were to some degree influenced by Rubens. But these, alongside the great master, were limited in their range and remained merely specialists.

By far the most talented pupil and collaborator of Rubens was *Anthony Van Dyck* (1599–1641). In contrast to the red-blooded, manly work of his master, Van Dyck's work is finer, more sensitive, and more feminine, with a distinct tendency toward the courtly and refined. Van Dyck went to England twice: first in 1620 to paint a portrait of King James I, and again, after a few years spent in Italy and Antwerp, to become court painter to Charles I, by whom he was knighted in 1632. Moving further and further away from the Flemish tradition, he developed his own charming style of portraiture and discovered a way to paint the nobility inimitably and with great taste. In the end, his art became a bit bloodless and overrefined; yet his influence on the great English portrait painters of the eighteenth century–Gainsborough, Romney, and Lawrence–is stronger than on the painters in his own Netherlands.

One of the few painters who remained uninfluenced by the Italians was *Adriaen Brouwer* (1606?–1638), who died in Antwerp at the age of thirty-two. In pursuing his own way he reminds us of Bruegel. He is sometimes placed in the Dutch School because he worked in Amsterdam and Haarlem and knew Frans Hals. Brouwer was a wanderer, always without money, the precursor of the nineteenth-century garret Bohemian. In his raw scenes of life in the inns, of smoking, drinking, and fighting peasants, he has painted pictures of low passions, in sharp contrast to the complacent paintings of Sunday peasants by Teniers and Van Ostade. The harshness of his scenes is mitigated by the soft sensitive colors, the grays and browns, the flowing brush strokes, and the masterful chiaroscuro. Most of his works, among which are a few mood landscapes, are in Munich. Rembrandt and Rubens appreciated him highly and owned many of his paintings.

SPAIN

Spain, like the Netherlands, experienced the highest flowering of its painting in the century of the Baroque. Half a century after El Greco came *Diego Velázquez* (1599–1660), and these two great artists present quite a contrast. El Greco is the visionary; Velázquez, the sharp observer of reality. With Velázquez there is no trace of mysticism, not even in his religious works. A master of the free, broad brush stroke and the direct, spontaneous reproduction, he was not a draftsman but a great colorist—one who can be compared to his Dutch contemporary, Frans Hals. Both Hals and Velázquez were favorite painters of Manet and the other French Impressionists (as El Greco was a favorite of the later Expressionists). Both painters were well-nigh equals in sharp observation and showy brush strokes, but Velázquez had a much stronger feeling for style than did Hals.

Above all, Velázquez was a portrait painter. In 1623 he became court painter to Philip IV, and in his studio in the palace he created numerous paintings of the king and queen, princes and princesses, court officials, and court dwarfs. His "Infanta Margarita with a Vase of Flowers" lacks the childlike qualities and the warmth which other painters put into their children's portraits. The little blonde princess poses stiffly and ceremoniously, properly aloof in an attitude demanded by the severe etiquette of the Spanish court. But we forget all this because of the masterful technique and the indescribably refined color: the pink and silver of the dress with its black lace, the blonde hair, and the tender, transparent skin against the background of a warm, dark red and black Turkish rug and a green-blue tablecloth, on which stands a small vase of flowers. The figure of the child is as light and flowery as the pale red roses, which might have been painted two centuries later by Manet.

It has been said before that the artistic value of a historical painting is not very high, and that such works are rarely masterpieces. The paintings of sieges and land and sea battles are

Fig. 33—DIEGO VELÁZQUEZ: *Surrender of Breda. Ca.* 1635. Prado, Madrid.

comparable to present-day news photos and are produced by minor talents. However, in the "Surrender of Breda" (Fig. 33) Velázquez has painted a work of extraordinary artistic quality. In 1590 the town of Breda in Holland was taken by Maurice of Nassau. In 1625 it was recaptured after a siege of almost a year by the Italian general Spinola, who served as commander of the Spanish army. The news of the surrender was received with great joy in Madrid. Impressed by the very brave defense of Justin of Nassau, Spinola allowed the surviving members of the garrison to retreat with honor, flags flying and drums sounding. Spain was not too happy about the honor accorded the heretic enemy, but Velázquez has chosen precisely this courtesy as his theme.

In the painting the capitulation takes place on a small hill which in reality does not exist. On the left stands a small group of Dutchmen and on the right, a larger, more compact group of Spaniards, whose mass effect has been strengthened by

Spinola's brown horse and a forest of long perpendicular lances, which gave the painting the popular name of "Las Lanzas." This motif is not new (it is also found in a Dutch painting of 1610), but nowhere else has it accented so much the power of a victorious army. The two main figures step forward. Justin offers the keys of the fortress with a deep bow, and Spinola puts his hand on his shoulder as if to say, "You have fought bravely; better luck another time." In the middle background, above the heads of these two figures, the defeated garrison marches off flying the orange, blue, and white flag. Still farther away we can see clouds of smoke rising from fires and drifting over the blue-green flat country with the town of Breda and the river Mark. Velázquez accentuated not the destructions of war but the best virtues of the warrior: homage paid to courage. Obviously it was to be expected that the Spanish victory was a proud moment. But there is more in the painting than pride. It does not express the spirit of *vae victis* (woe to the vanquished), but rather the respect accorded a vanquished opponent. The court painter Velázquez, so much a painter that we hardly know him as a human being, has included his own portrait on the far right.

Whereas Velázquez was a favorite of the Impressionists and El Greco of the Expressionists, *Bartolomé Esteban Murillo* (1618–1682) was admired especially by the Romantics. Like Velázquez, Murillo came from the warm climate of Andalusia in Southern Spain and worked in Seville. Compared to the manly and solemn art of Velázquez, however, Murillo's style is sentimental and feminine, the artistic relationship could be described as similar to that between Rubens and Van Dyck.

Murillo was a charming painter, and in his religious works he tended toward the lovely and gracious. His favorite subject was the Virgin Mary, the "lovliest of women," enthroned in clouds, and the models for his Madonnas were the handsome dark-eyed Andalusian women. His paintings of Sevillian children are also well known, especially the "Beggar Boys throwing Dice" (in the Alte Pinakothek in Munich). If we compare one of his idealized beggar boys with a fisherman's child by Frans Hals, we find that Hals has portrayed his subject realistically, whereas Murillo gave his child an angelic appearance in spite of the child's torn clothes.

Murillo belongs to the Counter Reformation, and in him we find the Baroque characteristics: movement, the chiaroscuro effects, spaciousness, and drama. But the vitality and strength of the Baroque has waned in his paintings to a soft coquettishness already proclaiming the eighteenth century.

FRANCE

France, like Spain, played only a modest role in painting before the seventeenth century. In the century of the Baroque, however, some great masters came forward, although they did not attain the stature of Rubens, Rembrandt, or Velázquez.

Nicolas Poussin (1594–1665), although Baroque in his style, still belongs in spirit to the Renaissance. A great admirer of Raphael and of antiquity, he spent most of his life in Rome, and his "Et in Arcadia Ego" (Fig. 34) is evidence of his admiration. In this painting a group of Greek shepherds, three men and a woman, is examining an inscription on an antique tomb which reads: "Et in Arcadia ego" ("I too was in Arcadia"). The figures

Fig. 34—NICOLAS POUSSIN: *Et in Arcadia Ego.* 1638–39. Louvre, Paris. (Archives Photographiques, Paris)

are symmetrically arranged, and like beautiful statues they seem to be composed in one plane, without depth, and placed against the stone of the tomb like sculptured Greek high relief. The beautiful, carefully considered attitudes and the arrangement of the draped garments disclose Poussin's close study of both the statues of antiquity and the paintings of Raphael.

Poussin was a reasoning and careful builder. His art was classic in its conception and devoted to antiquity and was the basis for the formal French academic tradition, for in his day the pure drawing of his figures and the grandeur of his compositions were especially esteemed, and it seemed proper that all art should be bound by fixed rules which could be taught and would produce similar results.

Poussin brought something new to landscape painting. Imposing his view of classical order upon nature, he produced forms which measure the space they penetrate. This quality, which closely borders on abstraction, has often been compared with music. Whereas the Renaissance gave the landscape only a limited range, the Baroque set it loose into space, and Poussin infused it with harmony.

Owing to the clarity, the order, poetic content, and rhythmic structure of his paintings, Poussin has always been much appreciated in France. Temperamentally, he was typically French, and was greatly admired by Cézanne and Degas.

We find this interest in the landscape with the great Dutch painters Van Goyen, Ruisdael, Seghers, and with the second great French painter of the seventeenth century, *Claude Lorrain* (real name Claude Gellée, 1600–1682), who, like his friend Poussin, spent most of his life in Rome. Claude was exclusively a landscape painter. With him the landscape has been shorn of any accidental realism. It has been idealized and adorned with Greek temples and other antique buildings. Thus, the landscapes of Poussin and Claude are called "heroic landscapes." Unlike Poussin, Claude cared little for his figures, which are incidental. He was interested mainly in the expression of immeasurable space in an atmosphere suffused with light. He liked to paint mornings and evenings and even dared paint the sun, something which Dirk Bouts had already done around the year 1460.

Two centuries after Claude, the atmosphere and light of the Impressionist paintings recall the effects which Claude achieved. Comparison, however, reveals a far greater dramatic quality in Claude's landscapes. He combined elements of naturalism with poetic intensity. It is the lyric qualities of his works which have endeared him to idealistic periods.

Only recently has interest in some painters from the French Baroque revived. The three brothers *Le Nain* (Antoine, Louis, and Mathieu) had for a long time been well-nigh forgotten. Hailing from Laon and working in Paris, they did not adopt the classicism of Poussin and the court painters, but became genre painters. *Louis Le Nain* (1593–1648), the most important of the three, painted with a wide brush in grays and browns and chose subjects from peasant life—for example, "The Hay Cart."

An even more recent discovery is *Georges de la Tour* (1593–1652), who worked in Lorraine, outside the great art centers. His paintings of religious scenes contain few figures and are characteristically presented in a night setting. His source of light was a torch or candle held by one of the figures, and the strong chiaroscuro is the most striking element of his rare paintings. With their mystical atmosphere and simplified concise form they are unique in the classical French Baroque tradition and singularly "modern" in their conception.

12

The Golden Age of Dutch Painting

(*1600–1680*)

The Union of Utrecht in January, 1579, completed the political separation between Northern and Southern Netherlands. Henceforth, the two countries would go their own way politically. There was a divergence in their artistic paths also, although some contact did remain. The differences between the art of the North and that of the South became strongly pronounced in the seventeenth century. The South, dominated by Rubens, was marked by the movement, pathos, and dashing ostentation of the Baroque. In the North, these qualities seemed alien to the outwardly sober style of the Dutchmen, who, averse to pompousness, tended more toward the contemplative. In Holland, the Baroque had a limited influence, although certain characteristics of that style, such as unbounded space and chiaroscuro, are found in Dutch art.

Generally, one can describe Dutch art of the seventeenth century as bourgeois and realistic. Perhaps it is better to say "bourgeois and *thus* realistic." In a culture where the businesslike middle class sets the cultural tone (as was the case in Europe during the nineteenth century), realist art carries the day. Eighteenth-century Holland was the first state in modern history ruled by a "bourgeois" class. It was the merchant, the industrialist, and the shipowner—not the Church, the Court, or the nobility (as in Spain, France, Italy, and Flanders)—who commissioned and bought paintings. It was they also who determined taste in the world of art. The bourgeoisie were at this time full of vigor and enterprise, and not without feeling for art; nevertheless, their artistic taste sought that which was understandable and familiar. Customers wanted portraits of themselves, alone or with their families, or as members of the guards or regents of a guild or an institution; they wanted pictures of their wives and children, of the interiors of their homes and of their countrymen at play. A throng of painters, with a technique that approached perfection, put all these things on canvas, and it is a unique phenomenon that in such a limited area mainly the three provinces of North Holland, South Holland, and Utrecht—such a large number of excellent painters were at work. The public bought the paintings, and visiting foreigners were amazed at the number of paintings privately owned.

The painter-critic Eugène Fromentin, referring to these masters, said in his book *Les Maîtres d'autrefois* (1876), "Il était dans la destinée de la Hollande d'aimer ce qui ressemble" ("It was the destiny of Holland to love likenesses"). The Dutch painters *were* realists. It was not religious, mythological, or allegorical ideas but visual reality which they portrayed; their art was born out of the joy of reproducing what delighted the eye. There are, to be sure, exceptions; Rembrandt's art was certainly based on something more than the re-creation of appearances. But the pathetic, so-called sublime, and grand manner of the Baroque style did not become popular. When commissions were given that *did* call for the more lavish style—for example, when the Orange Hall in the House Ten Bosch was to be decorated with allegories—a Fleming of Rubens' school, Jacob Jordaens, was designated.

It should not be assumed, however, that Dutch painting represents an art of a lower order because daily life is its subject. The value of a painting is determined not by the subject matter, but by the way in which the artist has expressed his own concept of life in the work. Dutch painters, with all their realism, have not given us photographic images. In the first place, their composition is careful and balanced, and they have a refined feeling for color. Not visual reality alone, but a certain attitude toward life is the basis of their work; it reflects a feeling of intimacy and quiet rejoicing in everyday things. With the exception of Rembrandt, we do not find any drama. What we do discover is a pronounced optimism, adopted later by the nineteenth-century

French Impressionists. This view might be sober as with Gerard Dou or Van der Helst, but it could also rise to the poetic and the meditative, as with Vermeer, or to the exalted, as with Ruisdael.

Dutch painting of the seventeenth century is characterized by specialization. Except for the versatile Rembrandt, Dutch artists for the most part confined themselves to particular subjects—still life, portrait, landscape, or genre.

THE STILL LIFE

Nothing is more characteristic of seventeenth-century Dutch art than still-life painting. Lacking all action and story quality, the still life concentrates on the world of inanimate matter. A contemplative, undramatic attitude characteristic of many Dutch painters may account for their affinity for the still life and may further explain why interior settings by Terborch, Pieter de Hooch, Vermeer, and others, also have a still-life appearance.

At first sight the concentrated little paintings of the Haarlem painters *Pieter Claesz* and *Willem Claesz Heda,* who worked in

Fig. 35—PIETER CLAESZ: *The Pitcher* (detail). 1627. Collection of Count van Lynden. (Courtesy B.K.D. The Hague)

the first half of the century, are not impressive and could be easily ignored. They are mainly "little snacks"—a corner of a table with the tablecloth pulled back and covered with tin plates, ham or cake, a half-peeled lemon, or a glass of wine. The local color is suppressed in favor of an almost monochromatic color—grayish green or gray-brown. After careful observation one discovers how finely balanced are the sober hues and the accents of light and dark.

Pieter Claesz's "The Pitcher" (Fig. 35) is no mere imitation. The pitcher, an everyday article, mirrors a world in its gleaming surface and is depicted with feeling and depth. Through the painter's vision, the prosaic has acquired something monumental and has become a thing of beauty.

Around the middle of the century the still life became richer both in choice of subject and in composition and color, a development which may be attributed to the increasing prosperity of the bourgeoisie and to the influence of the Baroque. Instead of the plain pewter utensils, we see silverware and mother-of-pearl shells on gilded pedestals; rugs from China and the Near East replace the white tablecloth. Strong color replaces the monochrome, while the fine binding hues and chiaroscuro are retained.

In this flowering period of Dutch art, from around 1635 until 1665, the most important master of the still life was *Willem Kalf* (1622–1693). With Kalf the still life reached its finest form. In his works the still-life objects seem to glow with a new intensity—achieved through the binding effects of light and color. From the depth of a dark background the magic of the light develops in a manner similar to Rembrandt; it slides across the Baroque curves of his silver tankards and reflects mysterious light flickers in the golden and glass drinking cups. The silver tankards, the blue Ming vases, golden oranges, and gleaming red Persian rugs form a harmony of colorful splendor.

While a still life ordinarily has no spiritual purpose, the *vanitas* still life does have a symbolic meaning. (The term *vanitas* is derived from the passage from Ecclesiastes: "Vanitas vanitatum, omnia vanitas"—"Vanity of vanities, all is vanity.") Such still lifes serve as reminders of the brevity of human life; a skull, an hour glass, a partly burnt candle, and a broken glass suggest the transitoriness of life. The *vanitas* still life, mainly a specialty of Leiden, probably flourished under the influence of Leiden University, a center of theological studies.

THE PORTRAIT

Frans Hals (1580?–1666), the first great master of the Dutch "Golden Age" and one of its finest painters, has become famous especially through nine great works of corporations, guards, and regents, of which eight are now in the Frans Hals Museum in Haarlem and one in Amsterdam. With Hals the artificiality and formality of collective portraits has changed into a loose natural group picture, a lively alternation of standing and sitting figures and light and dark color planes. Space and atmosphere surround the figures, who have been placed in their own proper social milieu. Hals did not follow the careful process of delineation used by his contemporaries; freer and more daring, he merely indicated the forms with sketchlike brush strokes, putting colors together without transition. The result is a "shorthand" of striking directness (which creates the painting, so to speak, under our very eyes). Two centuries passed before this technique was applied again—this time by Manet and the other nineteenth-century French Impressionists, the followers of Hals and Velázquez.

In 1664, at the age of 83, Frans Hals painted his last two groups: "Regents of the old Men's Home" and the "Women Governors of the Haarlem Almshouse," now in the Frans Hals Museum in Haarlem. Frans Hals was then a pauper living on public charity. Gone was the gaiety of his younger years. The rich colors of his earlier work had given place to grays and black; yet within these dark hues a single touch of color, like the red of a book on a table, stands out strongly. In these final pictures a pessimistic artist sees man as a lonely being. Hals painted these regents at the end of their lives, alone and without ties.

It has been said that these paintings were done impressionistically, but with an expressionistic character. As the testimony of an old man who looked beyond the superficial appearances of life, they are truly among the most moving of paintings. Hals's "Portrait of Nic Hassalaer" (Fig. 36) has the spontaneity of life. Here, too, are the broad brushstrokes of the *alla prima* technique.

Fig. 36—FRANS HALS: *Portrait of Nic Hassalaer. Ca.* 1627. Rijksmuseum, Amsterdam.

Brusquely and carelessly this figure is placed at an angle, turning toward the spectator—an attitude which was supposed to be balanced by the portrait of his wife.

The art of Frans Hals is visual and not intellectual. His works lack the spiritual depths of an artist like Rembrandt, so that the critic might hesitate before placing Hals among the few very great painters. Nevertheless, he was unsurpassed in capturing the fleeting moments of life.

THE LANDSCAPE

Landscape painting reached its high point in the Netherlands and not in Italy. In Italian art, the heir of Greece and Rome, Man occupied the center; the landscape served only as background. The Dutch landscape painter removed Man from the central position and allowed the landscape to dominate him.

In seventeenth-century Holland the first great European landscape school originated. During this period a number of painters recorded their images of Holland—the sea and dunes, the rivers, the woods, the towns, and the countryside. An important step in the evolution of pure landscape is marked by a new kind of composition. The multiplicity of the images of the preceding century was bound into an organized unity. The painter, no longer mainly concerned with separate details, became chiefly interested in the whole, in space, and in the atmosphere. He found new means to create the illusion of distance.

In Dutch landscapes there is a humility toward the unbounded nature which dominates Man. Perhaps this feeling can be explained by the distinctive character of the Dutch countryside, in which there is no sharp delineation, and where the fields, the sea, and the skies flow away into endless space. The air, the intangible element, becomes all-important. The atmosphere, saturated with water vapor, softens the contours; it blurs the colors and gives an impression of limitlessness. The artist's real purpose was to suggest this feeling of space and atmosphere rather than to depict the local topography. The creation of a pure landscape art, one of the foremost contributions of Dutch painting, is even more remarkable in that those landscapists greatly influenced the painters of other countries, perhaps even more than did Rembrandt or Vermeer. The nineteenth-century landscape in England and France, for instance, is unthinkable without such Dutch predecessors as Van Goyen, Ruisdael, Hobbema, and Cuyp.

We can distinguish roughly three stages in the development of the seventeenth-century landscape. In the first stage, which lasted until 1630, the landscape still has the character of an illustration; it is more a drawing than a painting, and the local, or inherent, color of each object is strong. The customary sixteenth-century division into three color planes of brown, green, and blue is still evident. To the group of painters working in this way belong *Hendrick Avercamp* and the seascapist *Hendrick Vroom.*

In the next stage, the story element has vanished. Expression of space, air, and atmosphere is the main goal. The local color becomes a grayish monochrome, and the drawing gives way to

Fig. 37—JAN VAN GOYEN: *Two Oaks.* 1641. Rijksmuseum, Amsterdam.

painting. This transition from the colorful to gray and atmospheric tones may be seen in works by the landscapist *Jan van Goyen* (1596–1656), who in his "Two Oaks" (Fig. 37) clearly departed from the detailed illustration of the first period. The two mighty trees, tortured by the elements, stand on the hill against a dark, stormy sky. From the hill in the right foreground the land stretches out, slowly changing in color as it extends toward the far horizon. The vision of the landscape is wide, impressive, and romantic. The people there are unimportant and appear to be suspended in space. Because of their small size, they convey the same feeling of limitlessness as does the white bird against the dark sky. The horizon, which once would have been delineated by trees and houses, has lost itself in infinity. Color has been limited to the modest gamut of browns, grays, and greens, accented by the red and blue of the human figures. The spaciousness of the painting is enhanced by the Baroque diagonal.

The rare landscapes of plains and mountains of *Hercules Seghers* (1590–1638) are even stronger images of the loneliness and limitlessness of space. Compared with his realistic-minded contemporaries, Seghers was a fantast and a visionary, a lonely man appreciated only by the great Rembrandt, who felt spiritually akin to him.

In the third stage of landscape painting, from 1650 to 1670, the art reached its fullest flowering. A tendency toward stronger local

Fig. 38—JACOB VAN RUISDAEL: *Mill near Wijk.* 1665–69. Rijksmuseum, Amsterdam.

color, which remained subdued, fine in tone, and never gaudy, becomes evident; at the same time the effects of atmosphere and space are preserved. The greatest landscapist of the seventeenth century was *Jacob van Ruisdael* (1628–1682). Both a physician and a painter, Ruisdael seems to have been a lonely and melancholy man. His great panoramas of oak woods, forested hillsides with castles and ruins, rushing cascades, and stormy beaches are filled with the romantic and serious poetry of nature. Of all the

Dutch landscapists his vision is the most exalted one. His famous "Mill near Wijk" (Fig. 38) reveals his careful craft of landscape art. The mill, which still stands, makes a much different impression on the spectator who sees it in its natural surroundings than it does in the painting. In Ruisdael's conscious portrayal it rises higher, more monumentally against the towering clouds, dominating the scene. Using repeated diagonals and working with contrasts of light and dark, Ruisdael composed a stately image of nature, an artistic structure which creates a natural impression. In its monumental solemnity, this landscape is one of the most imposing in Dutch art.

Within the art of the landscape, several specialties developed. The sensitive *Aert van der Neer* painted the quiet poetry of the moonlit night and of the winter. *Aelbert Cuyp* drenched his scenes with golden sunlight. *Paulus Potter* and *Adriaen van de Velde* chose the landscape filled with animals, while Adriaen's elder brother, *Willem,* made the sea his specialty. This was the time, too, of a special genre: the town view, represented by the Haarlem brothers *Job* and *Gerrit Berckheyde* and the Amsterdam painter *Jan van der Heyden.* The most beautiful work of this type, the "View of Delft" now in the Mauritshuis in The Hague, was the work of a nonspecialist, Jan Vermeer. Its strong color and intensity of light make this a work of genius, unique for its time.

REMBRANDT

Dutch art would not be accorded its very high rank in the history of art if, along with so many fine but doubtlessly limited painters, one man had not appeared who was to stand out among all others. This artist, *Rembrandt van Rijn* (1607–1669), elevated Dutch realism out of the atmosphere of daily life and security into the sphere of the universally human. He did not rise above the rest because of technical virtuosity, for he shared that with many others. His work is unique in that it probes profound spiritual depths, which is the secret of truly great art. We look at his contemporaries with pleasure, but we approach Rembrandt with awe, for we are drawing near Man's soul. Rembrandt was strongly subjective. In his portraits, especially in the later ones, he infused his subjects with an inner life which had its source in his own creative genius. His aversion to flattering beautification and slavish imitation of superficial appearances sometimes led to models' objecting that "they did not look like that."

In these few pages we can only give a brief review of Rembrandt's art. The enormous task facing the modern critic who would devote himself to an exhaustive study of Rembrandt is truly overwhelming when we realize that the artist produced more than 600 paintings, 275 etchings, and 2,000 drawings.

In his early days in Leiden, Rembrandt was a refined painter. The paintings from this period—with their enamel-like smoothness and subtle grays, purples, and blues—are superb. In these small, carefully executed canvases he studied and worked out problems of light and shadow; in these paintings a strong light produced by a burning candle or the sun was concentrated on the main figure: a money changer or a scholar engrossed in his papers. Such early experiments are important to his later works, in which light plays a central role. These first studies evidence the birth of the "Rembrandt principle": the dramatic light which shines out of the surrounding darkness. "Simeon in the Temple" (in the Mauritshuis in The Hague) can be considered the crowning glory of these studies. Here the main group is bathed in a light which has no visible source. In Rembrandt's works, the chiaroscuro has a totally different effect from that once used by Caravaggio to heighten the clarity and realism of his subject; here, it unifies the psychological interpretation, provides an atmosphere both dramatic and mysterious, and enhances the profound human values and spiritual meaning.

As a young but already acknowledged master, Rembrandt went to the prosperous merchants' town of Amsterdam. In the beginning he worked mainly as a portraitist. An important commission entrusted to him in his second year there, "The Anatomy Lesson of Dr. Tulp" (a group portrait of the Amsterdam Guild of Surgeons), is evidence of his success. Several elements contribute to the unity of this composition—the binding force of the chiaroscuro and a triangularly closed structure. In addition, an inner unity exists in the relationship of surgeons to each other and to their work: they are spiritually bound together by their common interest in the demonstration and the lecture.

Fig. 39—REMBRANDT VAN RIJN: *Syndics of the Cloth Guild*. 1662. Rijksmuseum, Amsterdam.

Three more times Rembrandt contributed corporation pieces. One of these, "The Anatomy Lesson of Dr. Joan Deijman," was largely destroyed by fire and only a fragment is left. The other two, "The Night Watch" (1642) and "The Syndics of the Cloth Guild" (1662), have been considered, along with "The Anatomy Lesson of Dr. Tulp," as milestones in the master's development.

In "The Night Watch" (in the Rijksmuseum, Amsterdam) the traditional manner of portraiture has been set aside. The personality of these guards had to be minimized so that they could be shown as a corps. Answering the order of their captain, they have streamed out of the dark gate into the clear sunlight and prepare to line up for a march through town. Rembrandt has added some extras—a little street Arab, two girls dressed in yellow, and a dog barking at the drummer. Thus, he has created a lively and disorderly scene which will rearrange itself into a pattern upon the captain's command. Pictorially, however, Rembrandt's interest is in the light and color, the harmonious decorative distribution of light and shadow, where the light figures of the girls balance the light clothes of the lieutenant. In its orchestration, color is subdued in the shadows and intense in the sunlight; the alternation of dark and light is the dominant theme. Such an important commission as "The Night Watch" is a great painter's dream, but the finished work was a disappointment for most of the patrons, each of whom had to pay the large amount of one hundred guilders for his likeness. Unlike those artists who concentrated upon the details of each face and each costume and who so easily satisfied the customers, Rembrandt stood above literal and ingratiating portrayal.

In his "Syndics of the Cloth Guild" (Fig. 39) Rembrandt, now older, wiser, and more willing to obey the wishes of his clients, painted representative portraits; yet he found a new and original way to satisfy the traditional requirement of equal emphasis for each member of the guild. The syndics are shown not in their usual deliberation but as they account for their actions to us, the spectators. This painting stands as a monument of solidarity, a high point in the art of portraiture. The loosely rhythmic composition, the warm color, the glowing red of the tablecloth, the lined faces full of character, and the great simplicity and truth transform this into one of the most perfect portrait paintings.

Fig. 40—REMBRANDT VAN RIJN: *Saul and David*. 1660. Mauritshuis. The Hague. (Photo: A. Dingjan)

Besides the portrait, biblical subjects assume the most important place in the work of Rembrandt, and the large compositions of this kind from his later years are among the most moving paintings in existence. In his "Saul and David" (Fig. 40) Rembrandt did not choose the dramatic moment in which King Saul, moved by an evil spirit, wanted to kill the shepherd boy David with his spear; instead he selected the moment of inward struggle and resolution, when David with his music banished Saul's madness and made him weep. The spear has fallen from the king's powerless hand, and he has seized a dark curtain to wipe away his tears. Perhaps no other painting has shown so strikingly the liberating influence of music on the soul. The expression which has replaced Saul's madness eludes description. In this composition Saul sits on his high throne; at his feet the shepherd boy, completely engrossed in his playing, plucks the strings with swift fingers. The gap between the two figures is bridged by the invisible, fluidic music. The line of the king bends inward and corresponds to the outward thrust of the player and his instrument. One can say that the receiving element is balanced by the giving one. The play of light and color, the king's gaudy turban and the deep wine-red and gold of his cloak intensify the pathos and beauty of the moment. In contrast to Rembrandt's earlier work, this painting is impressionistic—yet not in the spirit of Frans Hals or the nineteenth-century Impressionists. With them the hand was directed by a sharp eye; with Rembrandt a soaring mind and a deeply spiritual nature are the prime movers.

Among Rembrandt's many pupils only one had the strength of mind to walk new paths: *Carel Fabritius* (1624?–1654), who died at an early age in an accident in Delft. Only a few paintings by Fabritius are known; nevertheless, he forms the chain between the two poles in Dutch art of the seventeenth century, represented by Rembrandt and Vermeer. It is also quite possible that Vermeer, ten years his junior, was his pupil in Delft. In the Mauritshuis in The Hague two interesting paintings by Fabritius are on view. One, the "Man in the Fur Hat," is close to Rembrandt in its composition. A small work, broadly painted in variations of brown, it is beautiful in its chiaroscuro and expression. The second, the famous "Goldfinch," is nearer Vermeer. Here, the Rembrandt principle of light center and dark background has been reversed. Against a white wall the little bird chained to a food tray is like a spot of dark color. Not only the masterly, tender touch but the sadness of the imprisoned goldfinch makes this painting particularly impressive. Fabritius' early death cut short a career which might have produced truly great works of art.

GENRE PAINTING

The genre piece presents an incident from daily life. It is not man's appearance which is portrayed, but his universality of experience, characterized by his daily actions and his surroundings. Although the genre painting is usually set in the interior, it may also take place in a court or in a garden, as with Pieter de Hooch. But even there, we find the closed, intimate atmosphere of the room.

The genre painting cannot be precisely described. At times it seems akin to the portrait; in Jan Steen's parties, for instance, there are portraits both of himself and his family. His "Poultry-Yard" in The Hague seemed for a long time so much a genre painting because of its setting that the critics did not realize the painting was intended as a portrait of the little girl in it and had been ordered as such.

At other times the genre painting comes close to the historical work. The difference is that historical paintings and portraits show specific persons and incidents while the genre painter portrays man as representative of his class, involved in everyday matters. The peasants in the inns are drinking and smoking; the maid is busy in the kitchen; a mother is taking care of her child; a lady is reading a letter or playing a musical instrument.

Generally, whatever the activity, there is an atmosphere of peace, as though the figures are completely happy in their surroundings. Only in the nineteenth century did art begin to illustrate the meaning of the words from Genesis—"In the sweat of thy face shalt thou eat bread"—by picturing labor as unpleasant or degrading.

Poverty, old age, and social conflict as presented later in the nineteenth and twentieth centuries are rare in the art of this period. Man in his happy and peaceful moments is seen playing or relaxing; the optimistic side of life prevails, and a painting of domestic sadness, like the "Sick Child" by Gabriel Metsu in the Rijksmuseum in Amsterdam, is rare.

If action and intensity are limited in these genre paintings, what, then, is the charm of these quiet images from daily life? In the first place, the charm is based solely on artistic values—on the smooth, perfect technique that reminds us of the fifteenth-century Primitives; on the faultless drawing, the tender observation, the carefully balanced composition; and on the colorful and yet subdued hues. In the second place, it is based on the feeling, the mood, the intimacy of the interior, and on our empathy with the figures in their peaceful and happy surroundings.

Of the many genre painters we shall mention only the most important ones. *Adriaen van Ostade* (1610–1685), a Haarlem painter from Brabant, was above all the painter of the peasant—

the peasant relaxing after his work, in a dingy inn with pipe and beer, while a local virtuoso tunes his violin. Whereas Rembrandt, especially in his later works, placed his figures in the foreground with little indication of space, Ostade merged his figures completely with their environment. Rembrandt, on the one hand, described conflict of souls without distracting details; Ostade, on the other hand, considered the dusky room with its gradations of light and dark nearly as important as the people. A painter of mood and intimacy, his scenes are heightened by a fine chiaroscuro—such as in his "Artist's Studio," where feeble light coming in from the left creates a dance of twilight hues and sensitive nuances which blur the people and objects in the dark corners. The origin of this chiaroscuro was probably Rembrandt, but Rembrandt's mysterious light effects have been weakened here to an atmosphere of romanticism and comfortable security. Despite his limitations, Ostade was a fine tonalist and a painter of balanced transitions flowing from light to dark in subdued hues.

Likewise a tonalist, but of more refined character, was *Gerard Terborch* (1617–1681), the only important painter from eastern Holland. Terborch's subjects were derived from the "upper classes," but he was also more distinguished and more stylish than the placid Ostade. Terborch regarded man more as an individual; thus he was an excellent portraitist, discriminating in his use of color, and a great lover of fine fabrics. The satin of a lady's dress, as in "Paternal Admonition," becomes a truly noble material through the reflected light which gleams on the pleats and wrinkles.

Gabriel Metsu (1629–1667) matured early and died relatively young. A pupil in the Leiden studio of Gerard Dou (a pupil of Rembrandt), he worked in Amsterdam and depicted the satisfied complacency of the bourgeoisie in the second half of the seventeenth century. Like Terborch, he was a strong colorist and a painter of fabrics; and his heavy Persian rugs, velvet, furs, and satin seem almost real. But there remains a striking difference between Terborch and Metsu: Terborch's satin is tight and gleaming; Metsu's is limp, heavier, and more flowing.

Pieter de Hooch (1629–1683), who worked best during his years in Delft, painted intimate domestic scenes and introduces us into the middle-class household to which he himself belonged.

He has probably painted his own Delft courtyards and houses, using his wife and daughter as models. A motif frequently used is the mother with her child in the quiet atmosphere of a late summer afternoon, when the low sunlight fills the room with golden rays. De Hooch liked to paint interiors in which the open door of one room gives a view of another. Light enters from two sides, and the fine gradations of direct and diffused light, of sun and heavy shadow, have been reproduced with great care. These interiors have been carefully composed in horizontal and vertical tones, and the structure of different light planes thus infuses the scene with great tranquillity. There is hardly any action; the quiet mood is all. The poetry of the home and the peace of the sunny afternoon are the artist's primary concerns.

Also from Delft was *Jan Vermeer* (1632–1675), one of the greatest painters of this fertile century. More versatile than de Hooch, Vermeer covered a wide range of subjects. Nevertheless, he is recognized by an often repeated motif—the woman in the interior.

In his "Milkmaid" (Fig. 41) Vermeer has apparently given us a daily incident with a minimum of action: a woman pouring milk. Nothing could be simpler. But Vermeer has seen this figure more deeply; and in his rendering of structure, color, and light he has elevated it to a monumental image. The composition is closed and massive; a diagonal runs from the still life along the right arm to the kerchief; and a vertical descends along the shoulder and hip. The solidity of structure gives this superb painting a completeness and a grandeur which make it seem much larger than it is. Vermeer's use of color has the same strength. The yellow bodice, blue apron, red skirt—the three primary colors—are enhanced by the green of the table cloth. The fierce yellow receives the strongest light, while the deep blue is introduced in the shadow; thus these colors achieve the most intense values.

Vermeer has risen above the imitation of visual impressions and has strengthened the form, intensified the color, and given matter a unique completeness; his work is larger than reality. The still life on the table—the basket, the bread, and the blue vessel (painted in dots, a technique called "pointillism" around the end of the nineteenth century)—is carefully calculated. As a matter of

Fig. 41—JAN VERMEER: *Milkmaid. Ca.* 1658. Rijksmuseum, Amsterdam.

fact the whole painting, even the figure with its downcast eyes, has a still-life character.

Vermeer, an emotional painter, was concerned with artistic matters—like pictorial structure and color—and not with spiritual matters as was Rembrandt. The differences between Rembrandt and Vermeer are striking. With Rembrandt the figures are light against a dark background; with Vermeer, we have a clear form against a light background. Rembrandt preferred warm colors, especially red and gold; Vermeer, cool colors, yellow and blue. As a craftsman in colors Vermeer can be compared with such artists as Cézanne and Mondrian.

Vermeer's mathematical mind naturally turned out paintings geometrically composed, constructed out of purely balanced parts. In one of his later paintings, "The Artist in His Studio" (in the Kunsthistorisches Museum, Vienna), only a few elements —the raised tapestry, the chair, the table, the painter turned slightly to the right, and the tiles curved toward the left—establish the space quickly. Penetration into depth is balanced by the horizontals of the ceiling and the map and by the verticals of the map and girl. Interplay between surface patterns and the illusion of depth are achieved through a delicate balancing of vertical, horizontal, and diagonal lines. The relationships are purely pictorial and based on composition and color, and each object is precisely ordered. Vermeer, typically Dutch in his use of subjects, had a stronger sense of style and clarity of construction than other painters, and his work has been truly called the "crystal" of seventeenth-century Dutch art.

Most Dutch genre painters were interested not in the story, the action, or the character but in the picturesque aspect of incident and atmosphere. There is one exception: *Jan Steen* (1626–1679). Steen was a born storyteller, a philosophical spectator and recorder of what is funny and foolish on the world's stage. To be sure, the role of raconteur made Jan Steen one of the most popular painters of his day. His art speaks through its subject even to those who have little feeling for painting. Steen, however, is more than a storyteller. In his best work he is also a great painter. Thus we have the rare case of works of art equally pleasing to the layman and the connoisseur. Some of Steen's works are quiet and subdued, but his boisterous feasts, drinking scenes, and comic incidents have given him the name of "the Dutch Molière." Children are seldom missing from his paintings and are characterized by an untouched naïveté; even in his wildest drinking scenes, they are shown as interested spectators. Steen was a master full of humor and zest, who stood with both feet in the midst of the Dutch life of his day. Neither a dramatist like Rembrandt nor a quiet searcher like Vermeer (although he approaches Vermeer in pictorial refinement), he takes his place alongside Frans Hals.

13

Rococo

(*1700–1789*)

During the eighteenth century, the seriousness, breadth, and pathos of the Baroque evolved into a more elegant and more playful style—the Rococo, in which decorative painting achieved its purest form. The style of the French drawing rooms, which avoided everything heavy, solid, and square, was characterized by an airy asymmetrical ornamentation of curls and shell shapes, called *rocaille* in French, and it is from this trait that the word "Rococo" is probably derived.

Each period of art may be viewed as the continuation of a preceding one and also as a reaction against it. In this sense Rococo may be considered a more refined Baroque. One can also point out the contrast between the two: the seventeenth century is manly, imposing, and grandiose; the eighteenth is frivolous, elegant, and ornate. Large, dark paintings were no longer suitable for the elegantly furnished rooms decorated in pastel shades or for the delicately carved, golden picture frames and ornaments. The Rococo spirit required paintings which were delicate in tone, frivolous in subject, and small in size. Many of them were incorporated into wall paintings to enrich the whole decorative scheme. Compared with the Renaissance and Baroque periods, in which the number of great artists was legion, the Rococo produced few masters who approached them in stature.

The panorama of eighteenth-century Rococo painting reveals important art centers in England, Venice, and France—which was to assume the leading role in art from that time onward.

Fig. 42—ANTOINE WATTEAU: *Embarkation for the Island of Cythera.* 1717. Louvre, Paris. (Archives Photographiques, Paris)

FRANCE

The works of *Antoine Watteau* (1648–1721) are probably the clearest expression of the Rococo. Born in Valenciennes, a Flemish town which had only recently been annexed by Louis XIV of France, Watteau was strongly influenced by the Flemish masters, especially Rubens. His "Embarkation for the Island of Cythera" (Fig. 42) is one of those *fêtes galantes* similar to the ones by Giorgione and Rubens. But Rubens' "Garden of Love" (in the Prado, Madrid) is robust and dynamic, whereas Watteau's "Embarkation for the Island of Cythera," the island of love where (according to myth) Aphrodite was born, is peaceful, the atmosphere poetic. In the distance Cythera rises out of the blue and pink haze, a fata morgana, alluring and yet unattainable. The procession of lovers moves like a garland of flowers adrift on the waves toward the waiting gondola surrounded by cupids.

Reflecting the romantic, lyrical spirit of a love song or a minuet of Mozart, Watteau's art expresses youth and joy; but Watteau had no part in all this himself. Weak and ugly, he lived in Paris in great poverty and suffered from an incurable disease. This perhaps accounts for the melancholy, autumnal mood which covers his work like a veil. Love and happiness lure us to the island of Cythera, but it is only a dream. After a brief period of success, Watteau died of consumption at the age of thirty-six.

With *Jean Honoré Fragonard* (1732–1806) and even more with *François Boucher* (1703–1770), the *fêtes galantes* became increasingly frivolous. Paintings by these two artists mirror the atmosphere of the light-hearted court of Versailles where Louis XV and his mistresses, Mmes. de Pompadour and du Barry, held forth. These artists painted wall paneling for the boudoirs of such ladies, and the erotic subjects were scarcely disguised by the mythological trappings. Boucher painted pastoral idylls and nudes; Fragonard, from Provence, never tired of depicting amorous situations.

In Fragonard's "The Swing" (Fig. 43) the Baroque has been raised to an extreme of elegance and airiness. The composition for the most part follows the lines of two crossing diagonals. The movement of the swing is accentuated by the countermovement of the adoring admirer on the ground. The trees in the park

Fig. 43—JEAN HONORÉ FRAGONARD: *The Swing*. 1766. Wallace Collection, London. (Reproduced by permission of the Trustees of The Wallace Collection)

flow in weak curves and lose themselves in the clouds of the background. Amidst this weightless world, a doll-like Rococo figure soars high above; her flounces, fluttering in the wind, reveal a well-shaped leg and dainty foot. A little slipper flies off into the air. The sculptured cupids on the pedestals seem to be involved in this elegant piquant game, and the tight enclosure of leaves gives the entire scene the atmosphere of a boudoir.

Paintings of this type are intended as decoration. Because of their light colors, they were fitted extremely well to the Rococo drawing rooms with their white and golden panels and furniture coverings of pale-pink silk brocade. This is real French art in its lively grace, elegant presentation, and its adoration of Woman. A century later, with the Impressionist Renoir, we find something of the same spirit.

The art of Watteau, Boucher, and Fragonard was intended for the pleasure of aristocrats and rich bankers; it was not yet concerned with the sober life of the common man. (Only in the nineteenth century, after the Revolution, would French art acquire the bourgeois character which Dutch art had reflected two centuries earlier.) Nevertheless, there was signs heralding a new simplicity and naturalness. *Jean Baptiste Siméon Chardin* (1699–1779) did not paint amorous adventures but simple scenes from the life of the middle class in the style of Terborch, de Hooch, and Vermeer. As with these Dutch masters, we find in Chardin the same feeling for chiaroscuro and for the intimate atmosphere of the home. His presentation and color, however, are more refined and charming. In this essentially feminine era Chardin, too, was a painter of women, albeit women of a class different from those of Boucher and Fragonard. Still more attractive are his tasteful and simple still lifes. With their small touches of color, and their Vermeer-like glow, they are miracles of pictorial refinement.

Rococo, a reaction against Baroque, shunned all that was weighty and grandiose. Thus, the light, airy pastel was often preferred to oil. The most important eighteenth-century pastel painters were *Maurice Quentin de la Tour, Jean-Baptiste Perronneau,* the Swiss *Jean Étienne Liotard,* and the Venetian woman pastelist *Rosalba Carriera*—all portraitists.

ENGLAND

Eighteenth-century England, the last important European country to develop a school of painting of its own, achieved an art style which was technically perfect from the very beginning. The reason is that great masters from the continent—Holbein and Van Dyck, for example—already had worked in England and had prepared the way.

Fig. 44—Thomas Gainsborough: *Portrait of Mrs. Grace Dalrymple Elliott. Ca.* 1778. Metropolitan Museum of Art, New York. (Courtesy of The Metropolitan Museum of Art, Bequest of William K. Vanderbilt, 1920)

An important English artist who was certainly greatly influenced by Van Dyck was *Thomas Gainsborough* (1727–1788). He usually placed the subject for a portrait—the tall, isolated figure which embodied the English ideal—full-length on the central axis of the scene, free of the frame at top and bottom. The composition of his paintings is in strong contrast with that of the French portraits of the period; the latter are more severely built in a triangular shape with a wide base and the figure cut off at the knees.

Gainsborough's "Portrait of Mrs. Grace Dalrymple Elliott" (Fig. 44) has a typically English character. The lengthy form, hanging arm, and the fall of the clothes underline the vertical action. There is a rising movement in the painting achieved not by linear means but through the relationship of light and shadow and colors which flow into space. This is an aristocratic art, created for and stimulated by the upper classes; but unlike the portraits produced for the aristocracy of Italy, France, or Spain, which contain an air of hauteur, these figures are presented amiably and naturally.

Gainsborough's works also begin to convey an important characteristic of eighteenth-century art—the new love of nature, the "return to Nature" preached in France by Jean Jacques Rousseau. The English park with its scattered trees, whimsical ponds, and curving paths gradually began to receive more attention than the portrayal of gardens in geometrical patterns. To Fragonard nature was merely background; to the painters of English gentry, who often lived on large estates, the contact was closer. While nature remained for the most part background, England began to take the first steps forward in the portrayal of reality in nature, following Ruisdael, Hobbema, and Cuyp, the great Dutch landscapists.

William Hogarth (1697–1764) is, like Jan Steen, first of all a storyteller. But whereas Steen was only amused by the spectacle of human depravity, Hogarth sarcastically criticized the moral corruption of society, as for instance in his great series "The Rake's Progress." Fortunately, Hogarth was more than a moralist. In his delightful portraits, which represent some of his best work, he is a real painter. The well-known "Shrimp Girl," a worthy counterpart of Frans Hals's "Gypsy," is fresh and gay.

Sir Joshua Reynolds (1723–1792), first president of the Royal Academy of Art and a man of culture and erudition, belongs more to the Renaissance and the Baroque in artistic conception, although strongly influenced by the Venetians, Van Dyck, and Rembrandt. He was born into an educated family, and his position, which contrasted markedly with that of contemporary English painters, enabled him to capture the lofty pose and station of his subjects. His portraits display a harmonious composition, naturalness, and charm—especially in paintings of children such as the little "Lady Caroline Howard" in the National Gallery of Art, Washington, D.C.

VENICE

At the end of the long flowering of Italian painting in eighteenth-century Venice stands *Giovanni Battista Tiepolo* (1696–1770), a decorative painter possessing versatility and genius. With astounding ease and fine sensitivity he filled large walls and ceilings with his mythological and religious compositions. His frescoes are found not only in Venetian churches and palaces but also in the Royal Palace in Madrid and in the magnificent palace (formerly a bishop's residence) in Würzburg.

The art of the town view (*veduta*), painted in Holland by Jan van der Heyden and Gerrit Berckheyde, also flourished in Venice, but by the end of the eighteenth century, the economic and political power of the city was declining. Although Venice was dying, it expired in a festive way. From all over Europe tourists visited the city and took home little paintings of the Rialto, the Grand Canal, or the Piazza San Marco as souvenirs. In a series of fine drawings *Antonio Canaletto* (1697–1768) and his cousin *Bernardo Bellotto* recorded the architectural beauty of the city and the canals. The paintings by Tiepolo's brother-in-law, *Francesco Guardi* (1712–1793), are more impressionistic than those of his contemporaries. His brushwork is broader, and through light touches of color he has captured the sparkle of Venetian scenes.

14

Revolution

(1789–1820)

In France, Rococo art ended abruptly in the year 1789. The Revolution swept the ruling classes away and with them their art vanished also. The old culture was destroyed, and out of the chaos was born a new one. The ruled became the rulers, and the new ideals of society demanded a new form of art—one which was neither aristocratic nor Christian. The new revolutionary ideals echoed those of republican Sparta and the Rome of antiquity. Opposed to the frivolity of the Rococo, these ideals were heroism, manly will power, and self-sacrificing devotion to one's country.

DAVID

The interpreter of these ideals in art was the painter of the Revolution and, later, of Napoleon: *Jacques Louis David* (1748–1825). Gone are the powdered lords and ladies of the *ancien régime*. Instead, we now have the people and spirit of the Revolution—as, for example, "La Femme du Peuple," which portrays one of the peddler women knitting beside the guillotine and counting the falling heads of the hated aristocrats. With fierce and challenging eyes and a mouth opened for a curse, the figure seems to burst forth into action.

The "Oath of the Horatii" (Fig. 45) can be considered a manifesto of the art of the Revolution. Painted in 1784 in Rome, it was exhibited in 1785 (four years before the Revolution) in the

Fig. 45—JACQUES LOUIS DAVID: *Oath of the Horatii.* 1784. Louvre, Paris. (Archives Photographiques, Paris)

Paris Salon. In sharp contrast to the *joie de vivre* of Rococo, David in this work portrayed his compatriots as embodiments of courage, inflexibility, and civic virtue. The feathery art of Rococo has been replaced by an art of iron discipline. The Paris public was familiar with the history of the brothers Horatii from the tragedy by Corneille. The three brothers urged on by their father fought three enemy captains in order to save Rome from conquest. The disciplined image, not the subject, was new, as was also the seriousness, the hardness, the clarity, and the plastic structure. Instead of the picturesque vagueness of Rococo backgrounds, we see a bare, open space enclosed by three arches supported by unadorned Doric pillars. In front of these three arches are the three main groups: to the left, the three brothers in martial attitudes; in the middle, their father holding three swords; to the right, three weeping women. The composition is based on a repetition of calculated triangles, and the three groups, although strictly separated, are bound together by the diagonals. The colors are somber and metallic. Line and sculpturesque form have taken the place of the Baroque and Rococo color; intellect has replaced feeling. With David begins the style of severe form known as Neoclassicism, which will rule the early nineteenth century.

GOYA

In Spain, art seemed exhausted after Velázquez. Then suddenly a surprising genius, *Francisco Goya* (1746–1828), came forward—even as did El Greco after the Renaissance and Picasso in our own time. Not only was Goya the most brilliant painter of the eighteenth century, he was also a pioneer who paved the way for nineteenth-century art and strongly influenced it. Unlike David's metal-hard plastic form, Goya's painting is broad and without

Fig. 46—Francisco Goya: *Don Ramon Satue.* 1823. Rijksmuseum, Amsterdam.

detail. As a painter, Goya built on the tradition of the great masters such as Titian, Velázquez, and Rembrandt. But he added new elements, and his work anticipated Impressionism, Expressionism, and even Surrealism.

Goya's numerous portraits of the Spanish royal family and their surroundings (he was official court painter to Charles IV) and portraits of his own friends express, in their often cruel characterizations, an incisive view of man. The portrait of the judge, "Don Ramon Satue" (Fig. 46), painted at the age of seventy-seven, can be compared with some of the late works of Frans Hals. The broad painting has a somber color. The black costume and white shirt against the dark-gray background are enlivened only by the strong flesh color of the face and the pink of the waistcoat. This figure, demonstrating the new anti-aristocratic mood of the time, is no stately representation. The judge poses with his hands in his pockets, his hair in disorder, and his shirt unbuttoned, with an expression both defiant and embittered. Here stands a citizen of a new era!

The great Revolution is reflected nowhere more clearly than in Goya's etchings and in such paintings as "The Execution of the Rebels, May 3, 1808" (Fig. 47), a vehement protest against war, tyranny, and injustice. As a historical document it is of a kind very different from Velázquez's "Surrender of Breda." Whereas Velázquez was a clever stage director, creating a fictitious scene and glorifying a famous feat of arms and the gallantry of the conquering hero, Goya did not view war from a distance, nor does his cleverly composed work look contrived.

The "Execution of the Rebels" is just one example of how Goya participated intensely in the happenings of his day. In 1807, Napoleon's armies, commanded by Murat, entered Spain. On May 2, 1808, the wild rebellion by the people against the French troops broke out in Madrid. The rebellion was brutally suppressed and numerous prisoners, among whom were many innocent ones, were condemned to death by a military court and shot during the night outside the gate. Goya, in all probability, was an eye witness of these terrible scenes. Out of this devastating experience the artist re-created one moment of horror.

The painting is divided into two parts by a diagonal. To the left we see the victims: those already killed, those standing in

Fig. 47—FRANCISCO GOYA: *The Execution of the Rebels, May 3, 1808*. 1814–15. Prado, Madrid

front of the rifles, and the long line of those being driven to the place of execution. In this frightful scene there is no place for heroism and contempt of death. All resistance has been broken; fear and horror may be seen in the faces of the helpless, doomed people. One man, his shirt open, raises his arms in fury and offers his breast to the lethal bullets. It is probably no coincidence that this man with the outstretched arms looks like Christ on the Cross. The strong light of the large lantern falls on him. Sharp contrasts are created by the flickering light and the black shadows. To the right, the executioners, the pack-laden French soldiers, are shown merely as a row of parallel bodies, legs, rucksacks, and rifle barrels. These soldiers are not thinking and feeling beings but robots, parts of a relentless war machine. Against the background of a starless night sky, a group of dark buildings stands on a bare hill. The picture offers no hope, no consolation.

In this work Goya was not glorifying any national heroism as was David. The one figure, who momentarily conquers his fear, acts only in a sudden rage which is like a flame soon to be extinguished. Nor does Goya demonstrate the cruelty of the enemy. No, the soldiers act mechanically; they are under a tragic coercion. This painting is, rather, an outcry against the horror and senselessness of war. Velázquez and Goya both created major works on the subject of war. In neither work, however, was war glorified. Velázquez expressed the nobility of the warrior, but Goya was unable to do even this. He had something new to say, something which would be said a century later by his compatriot Picasso in a different, though no less penetrating, way in "Guernica" (1937).

15

Neoclassicism and Romanticism

(ca. *1800–1850*)

The numerous art currents of the nineteenth century developed in logical order only in France. While other countries, such as England, Belgium, Holland, and Germany, made important contributions, France took the lead and attracted the outstanding talent from other countries. It was in France during the first half of the century that the two movements—Neoclassicism and Romanticism—originated.

In essence, nineteenth-century Neoclassicism was a revival of the art of the Renaissance. Born of revolt against the frivolous and refined boudoir art of the Rococo, Neoclassicism, a style of severely controlled form, returned to the work of Raphael and the statues of antiquity for its inspiration. Originating with Jacques Louis David, who had studied at the Roman Academy, Neoclassicism extended its influence far into the nineteenth century. David, the official painter of republican ideals, was forced to leave the country when the Bourbons returned to the throne, and he died in Brussels. After him, *Jean Auguste Dominique Ingres* (1780–1867) became the accepted Neoclassic master, and his works—especially his portraits, such as the "Portrait of Comtesse d'Haussonville" (Fig. 48)—reflect a great sensitivity for personality. In them the classic concept of form is softened by the lyrical and rhythmic linear pattern.

Romanticism was a revival of the Baroque. In the art of painting, Romanticism substituted color, chiaroscuro, and movement for the clearly drawn plastic form. Politically, French Romanti-

Fig. 48—JEAN AUGUSTE DOMINIQUE INGRES: *Portrait of Comtesse d'Haussonville*. 1845. Frick Collection, New York. (Copyright, The Frick Collection, New York)

cism was in opposition to the reaction that followed the Revolution, an opposition which finally led to the revolutions of 1830 and 1848. Romanticism originated with the younger painters and came to the fore with *Théodore Géricault* (1791–1824), whose "Raft of the Medusa" (Fig. 49) is perhaps his crowning achievement. Eugène Delacroix, of whom we shall have more to say later, was the successor to Géricault and brought Romantic art to its greatest flowering.

The contrast between Neoclassicism and Romanticism can be briefly summarized: Neoclassicism is static. It is an art of compactness, tranquillity, and equilibrium, and the composition is closed—in other words, the image is completed within the borders of the picture. The cool colors emphasize rationality, and the subjects are often taken from Greek or Roman history and mythology. At the academies, drawing and painting were taught by means of statues from antiquity. Next to these, Raphael's works were the models to be imitated. Romanticism, on the other hand, is dynamic, moving, and filled with inner tension and restlessness. The composition remains open (that is to say the image continues outside the frame), and warm colors enhance the emotional and expressive qualities. The subjects are often taken from medieval history and from novels and poetry; in the landscapes, ruins of castles and exotic settings evoke images of distant times and places.

Technically, a Neoclassic painting is more drawn than painted: the forms are rendered in pure and perfect contours, the brushstroke is scarcely visible, and the surface is smooth and the light even and cool. Romantic painting, on the other hand, is above all painterly. Color is used emotionally and the contours lose themselves in space. The elements of composition are not line and form, but color and chiaroscuro. Compared to the smooth perfection of Neoclassicism, Romanticism makes a much less complete impression. Nevertheless, this vagueness is what moves our feeling and fantasy.

These contrasts were not new. In former centuries, too, there had been refined painters and bold painters, painters of the precise controlled form and painters of free, dynamic form—on the one hand, Memling, Holbein, Raphael, and Vermeer; and on the other, Rubens, Frans Hals, Velázquez, and Rembrandt.

Fig. 49—THÉODORE GÉRICAULT: *Raft of the Medusa.* 1818–19. Louvre, Paris. (Archives Photographiques, Paris)

Although in the history of art the words "Neoclassicism" and "Romanticism" belong to the first half of the nineteenth century, the attitudes which they represent may be found throughout all centuries. Thus, art in which emotion, dream, and fantasy are dominant is called "romantic," and the art of the severely controlled form is called "classic." French art alternately followed one tendency and then the other. Poussin was classic; Watteau was romantic. In Holland Vermeer and Potter were more classic; Ostade, Ruisdael, and Rembrandt, romantic.

The leader of Romanticism in France was *Eugène Delacroix* (1798–1863), a fiery, passionate artist. He looked for his subjects in history, and in the literature of Shakespeare, Dante, and the Bible. During a journey through North Africa, he discovered the romance of the Near East, of lion hunts, and of life in harems.

In "Liberty Leading the People" (Fig. 50) Delacroix glorified an event from his own days: the July Revolution of 1830. The image of the street fighting, the workers and students surrounded by the smoke of gunpowder, could be called realistic. However, the main figure is an imaginary, allegorical woman—La Liberté.

Fig. 50—EUGÈNE DELACROIX: *Liberty Leading the People.* 1830. Louvre, Paris. (Archives Photographiques, Paris)

Her captivating form, full of fiery spirit, fits quite naturally into the whole. In her, all action and enthusiasm are concentrated; she lifts the event above time and place and reveals its higher, inner meaning. Created to arouse patriotic ideals, this painting is a masterful statement. It does not attempt to express the outrages of war, as do Goya's works, and in this sense it remains a historical document—not a profound comment on humanity.

Whereas the Neoclassicists David and Ingres organized the picture plane through their draftsmanship, Delacroix organized it through an alternation of light and dark parts of the painting. With him color plays a large role; in "Liberty Leading the People" this is particularly striking. The white figure rises from the dark earthlike colors around the barricade, acts as the base of the composition, and forms a pyramid at the top of which the color reaches its highest intensity in the blue-white-red flag.

After a long period of decline, German art revived in the new flowering of the romantic spirit. In German Romanticism, however, there is no trace of the fiery spirit, the revolutionary ideals, typical of the French Romantics. In *Caspar David Friedrich* (1774–1840), the most important representative of German Romanticism, a mystical feeling was carried over into the landscape. If the human figure plays any role in it at all, it is only to emphasize the loneliness and infinity of nature. Friedrich's motifs were the sea, mountains, ruins, and cemeteries enveloped in snow, fog, or moonlight. As with the classicists, his brush stroke is smooth and scarcely visible. Whereas Delacroix's influence during the nineteenth century until the time of Van Gogh was enormous, the melancholic and introverted Friedrich was soon forgotten. Only in the beginning of the twentieth century was he rediscovered.

In spite of all their differences, the two major artistic currents of the early nineteenth century, Neoclassicism and Romanticism, have in common one thing: their flight from everyday reality. Both arose out of preceding styles and both continued to exist alongside each other in many variations. At the same time, another style began to take shape and in this one the bourgeois nineteenth century would find its most characteristic expression —Realism.

16

Realism and Impressionism

(ca. *1850–1890*)

The art of the early nineteenth century, which reflected on the one hand an intellectualized idealism (Neoclassicism) and on the other hand a dramatic emotionalism (Romanticism), was replaced in the second half of the century by an art dedicated to the common experiences of daily life: Realism. This is not to say that Realism was devoid of intellectual or emotional elements or that the preceding styles lacked contact with reality; rather, the emphasis and intent was shifted.

Realism rejected the historical and literary subjects of Neoclassicism and Romanticism and concentrated on visible reality, on the life of the common man, and above all on the actual landscape. The most important period of realistic art prior to the nineteenth century was the Golden Age of Dutch painting—an island in the sea of Baroque. This bourgeois, realistic art found its continuation in the highly commercial-minded nineteenth century, which had discovered the pictorial charm of daily life.

One of the most striking features of the development of Realism was the preoccupation with the landscape. Jean Jacques Rousseau had preached the "return to Nature" and held this up to humanity as a haven for those who rebelled against the artificiality of eighteenth-century culture. For centuries, the place to find consolation in the face of tribulation had been the Church. Rousseau proclaimed, however, that the Divine could be found in nature, and the German landscapist, Friedrich, approached nature with reverence. The less mystically inclined Realists regarded nature with a familiarity and delight and painted what they saw.

The new art of the landscape began around 1800 in England with John Constable's fresh views of nature. Constable's work, with its color based on direct observation of nature, had a profound effect on French art, especially upon Delacroix. Around 1830 a group of landscape painters began to congregate in the French village of Barbizon—Rousseau, Corot, Millet, Daubigny, Dupré, and others. The Barbizon School, as it was called, formed a bridge between Romanticism and Realism. These artists painted the *paysage intime* ("intimate landscape") from a romantic point of view, but with an immediacy and involvement which was to characterize Realism. Like the English landscapists, they turned to the old Dutch artists, especially Ruisdael, for their subjects—the dewy morning, the melancholy dusk, the serene moonlight, the threatening storm. The Dutch were objective; the Barbizon painters, essentially sentimental. For those who were born, or at least lived, in the metropolis of Paris, nature was liberation. Thus, these painters depicted for the first time the longing of the city-dweller for the forests, the beaches, and the fields.

The founder of the Barbizon School, *Théodore Rousseau* (1812–1867), discovered the village Barbizon in the 1830's at the edge of the forest of Fontainebleau, which was in those days a wild place. In 1849 Millet joined him there. Rousseau liked to paint the trees of the forest, particularly the oak. He saw these royal trees with their heavy foliage in a romantic way, as something conquering the centuries, ruling their surroundings, and offering shadow and protection to man and beast. He had a completely different vision from the later Impressionists to whom the tree was nothing but a spot of color; thus, he painted his trees against the sky in careful detail. Unfortunately, Rousseau's paintings have darkened considerably because he worked with paint containing asphalt. As a result, one of his largest works, "La Déscente des Vaches" (now in The Hague), is totally ruined.

Compared with Rousseau's stiff seriousness, the art of *Camille Corot* (1796–1875) is spontaneous and sunny. During a two-year stay in Italy, Corot absorbed the charms of the landscape, in which, it seemed, every rock and tree was defined with an almost geometric structure. Such impressions, along with an awareness of the classical principles of structure, combined to produce in his early works landscapes of bell-like clarity, simplicity of form, and carefully calculated balance. Corot was only loosely connected with the Barbizon group, but its influence may be seen in his later works in which the solid structure is replaced by a delicacy and airiness. His vision was poetic and his landscapes are often furnished with little nudes and dancing nymphs. The color in his early works captures the solidity of the Latin landscape and the lucid atmosphere; in his later works silvery blues and grays suggest the effects of the northern atmosphere. His method of dissolving his landscapes into sunlight and atmosphere, as in "The Bathers" (in the Louvre), puts him on the borderline of Impressionism.

Jean François Millet (1814–1875), one of the leaders of the Barbizon group, painted not the landscape but Man, and particularly the working man. The emphasis he gave his subject, the peasant working, was new in art. In the past, painters of peasant life—artists such as Bruegel, Brouwer, and Teniers—generally depicted weddings and fairs, drinking bouts and fighting. But theirs was a "collective" view; no emphasis was placed upon the individual as such.

In Millet's "Winegrower at Rest" (Fig. 51) we see an exhausted laborer who has paused for a moment. The figure is drawn in large, simple contours without distracting details, and all interest is strongly concentrated in him. His figure rises pyramidally against a vague background. The tired, almost animal-like head with dull, staring eyes and mouth, the angular body, and the sharply delineated hands and feet, do not reveal Millet as the sentimentalist he was in his famous "Angelus" (wherein he showed the piety of the peasant). The winegrower convincingly portrays the hardship of peasant life. Because of such paintings the middle class misjudged Millet and considered his works a glorification of the worker and propaganda for socialism, but Millet wanted only to paint the peasant earning his bread by the sweat of his brow. Vincent van Gogh admired Millet very much and carried on the latter's work in his peasant figures.

Fig. 51—JEAN FRANÇOIS MILLET: *Winegrower at Rest.* 1869. Museum Mesdag, The Hague. (Photo: Lichtbeelden Instituut)

Fig. 52—HONORÉ DAUMIER: *The Third-Class Carriage.* 1862. Metropolitan Museum of Art, New York. (The Metropolitan Museum of Art, Bequest of Mrs. H. O. Havemeyer, 1929. The H. O. Havemeyer Collection)

Whereas Millet and his Barbizon group stood outside of politics, the Parisian *Honoré Daumier* (1808–1879) worked in the middle of political and social agitation. Along with Millet, he was interested in Man; his subject, however, was not the peasant but the working and the lower middle-class Parisian. Daumier was the first to express in his works the modern phenomenon of an anonymous city-dweller, the mass man.

Originally a caricaturist, Daumier had to pay for his attacks on the Bourbon Restoration with a prison sentence. In both lithographs and paintings he used simple lines to create charged forms, and in this sense he is a pioneer of Expressionism. Some of his figures are a condensation of his own scorn for brutality and injustice. Others reflect his profound admiration for such quiet virtues as patience and courage. His figures, in spite of their small size, seem large and towering. They are monumental expressions of humanity, without benefit of adornment or idealization. "The Washerwoman" and "The Third-Class Carriage" (Fig. 52) typify Daumier's warm feeling for his subjects.

The art of *Gustave Courbet* (1819–1877) did away with the last vestiges of Romanticism. Courbet sought to divest his own art of all the sentimentality which the works of the Barbizon School continued. During the World Exhibition in Paris of 1855, Courbet exhibited forty of his paintings in a wooden barrack and put a sign above the door which read: *Le realisme, G. Courbet.* He declared that he knew "neither ideals, nor religion, nor a soul" and painted only what was visible and tangible. More versatile than Millet and Daumier, Courbet painted landscapes, nudes, and still lifes in the dark, heavy colors of the Baroque, creating beautiful tones and putting strong accent on volume. Whether he painted apples or a woman's body, everything was materialistic and solid, without a trace of poetry. Like Hals, Courbet was a painter who wanted to be only a painter. Nevertheless, he also had strong political inclinations. As one of the leaders of the Commune of 1871, he was held personally responsible for the destruction of a pillar commemorating the empire of Napoleon in the Place Vendôme, and for this he was condemned to pay the cost of restoration. The "Still Life: Apples" (Fig. 53), as well as several other works, was painted by Courbet in a Paris prison.

If we survey the development of art from the Neoclassicism

of David and Ingres to the Realism of Courbet, we realize that the former emphasis on line and drawing has evolved into a domination by tone and color. Delacroix and the Barbizon painters relied on this painterly technique. With the Barbizon group, this painterly technique was used to evoke mood; with Courbet it was a value in itself. All artists who were primarily draftsmen regarded Ingres as their master. All pure painters, however, were disciples of Delacroix and Courbet.

Fig. 53—GUSTAVE COURBET: *Still Life: Apples.* 1872. Stedelijk Museum, Amsterdam.

In the second half of the nineteenth century, Courbet's influence triumphed. The artists of the next generation, the Impressionists, were masters of color and followed Courbet's example—with one major difference. Whereas Courbet, worked in the dark colors of the Dutch and Spanish Baroque masters, the Impressionists cleaned their palettes radically of all dark "museum" colors and black shadows and, instead, used the light, sun-drenched hues of the open air.

In 1874 the Parisian painter Claude Monet (who will be discussed later) exhibited a painting entitled "Impression—Rising Sun." On the basis of this work, a critic called Monet and his followers "Les Impressionistes." Though intended as a term of ridicule, the word "Impressionism" quickly found acceptance and indeed aptly characterizes the essence of this art.

The difference between Realism and Impressionism can be briefly stated. In Realism the painter depicts man, nature, and objects after experiencing and carefully observing them. He knows that what he sees has substance, that it has local color, and that it has three dimensions; and he attempts to present all these things as convincingly as possible. In Impressionism the artist disregards this knowledge. He takes in the total picture quickly and re-creates the impression, not the three-dimensional form. The Realists observed one thing at a time, ignored the changing effects of sunlight, and tried to retain the local color and to preserve the unchangeable quality of the subject. The Impressionists, however, wanted to catch the passing effects of light, and that is why they painted in the open air. They loved the evanescent glow and shimmer of light over surfaces. They wanted to be all "eye." To them, the effects of light and color and outer appearance were more important than the things themselves. As Manet remarked, "The main figure in the painting is the light."

The Impressionists realized how difficult it was to reproduce the intense power of color in full sunlight. To achieve their effects, they mixed the colors as little as possible and put the unmixed colors on the canvas in little dabs which, when seen from a distance, flow together and give the desired result. Since light and shadow change so quickly because of the changing position of the sun, the Impressionist had to paint quickly, decisively, in a sort of "brush writing." His hand at times reacted so readily and accurately to the scene that nature seems to be caught as if in a photograph.

The Impressionists began with the landscape. Because the image was to be a general one, not detailed, and since this has to be achieved from some distance, landscape was the most suitable subject. Later, the Impressionist technique was used in the painting of the human figure and the still life. The masters of Barbizon were romantics in that they fled from the big city and looked for beauty in the lonely woods. The Impressionists, on the contrary, felt quite at home in Paris and accepted modern life without reservation. They painted the human masses on the boulevards, the rowers on the Seine River, the races in the Bois de Boulogne, the Parisians in their homes, and the gaudy world of festivals, the stage, the fair, and vaudeville; in their landscapes we see viaducts, railway stations, and trains. "Il faut être de son temps" ("One must live in one's time"), Manet said; and the French Impressionists have indeed left us an incomparably vivid image of the last thirty years of the nineteenth century, a vivid chronicle of bourgeois culture.

The forerunners of French Impressionism came early in the nineteenth century and are to be found in the Englishmen Constable and Turner and the Dutchman Jongkind. *John Constable* (1776–1837) was the first to give new expression to the nineteenth-century feeling for nature. At this time the English landscapists were still using the brownish colors which old Dutch paintings had acquired after their varnish had darkened with age (the so-called museum color). Through direct observation of nature Constable achieved in his fresh landscape studies a clear bright green, sparkling in the sunlight.

In "The Hay-Wain" (Fig. 54), the wagon crossing the ford, the farmhouse between the oaks, the figures, and the dog are merely sketched in. The most important element in the picture is the suggestion of weather, atmosphere, light and shadow, and space. Heavy storm clouds portend rain and wide shadows cover the landscape; yet flashes of sunlight hit the white walls, grass, and bushes and animate the scene. Little spots of color and of pure white have been placed on the canvas with the knife in order to indicate light on the waves and moisture on the grass. In technique, Constable was far ahead of his contemporaries, who were still influenced by the old masters. He did not look at nature with the eyes of others but rendered his impressions of the windy English landscape in a spontaneous way. He had to forget, he

Fig. 54—John Constable: *The Hay-Wain.* 1821. Victoria & Albert Museum, London. (Crown Copyright)

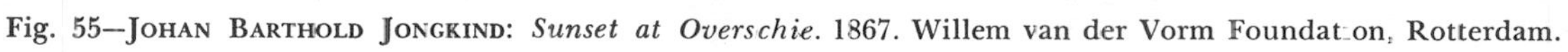

Fig. 55–Johan Barthold Jongkind: *Sunset at Overschie*. 1867. Willem van der Vorm Foundation, Rotterdam.

once wrote, that he had ever seen a painting. But he did not dare to place these so-called sketches (an inappropriate word because they express his intentions completely) on exhibition. He painted the same subjects again and in more elaborate detail, and these "completed" paintings he sent to the Academy, where they enjoyed great success. But the "sketches" he kept himself, and only later, when Impressionism had taught people to see differently, was the higher artistic value of these studies appreciated.

If Constable was a great forerunner of Impressionism, the same can be said of *William Turner* (1775–1851). His early works show a great veneration for the radiant sunrises of Claude Lorrain. But Turner went further in his rendering of sunlight effects than either Claude or Constable or any other painter before him. In the landscapes of Constable, the light gleams on the moist grass and glitters in the stream, but everything keeps its own substance; in the late works of Turner the solidity of material things is absorbed by light, mist, and cloud: fata morganas, where visions of cities and mountainous coasts float in a luminous haze. White sails rise up like ghosts out of a vaporous atmosphere; water and land flow together in orange and yellow hues. In such works as these Turner is a forerunner not only of Impressionism but of abstraction as well.

Johan Barthold Jongkind (1819–1891) began painting in the realistic and romantic manner of his master Schelfhout. In his later work the transition to Impressionism took place. In 1846 Jongkind went to France to live and work, but he frequently returned to the Netherlands, where he found the subjects for his paintings.

In the "Sunset at Overschie" (Fig. 55), towers, houses and trees, water, and the shore are all depicted in a playful, airy manner. Jongkind's main subject, the pervasive light, occupies the entire space and seems to turn solid matter into vapor. Everything is a play of reflections, transparent shadows, and touches of light which just barely indicate the form. Nevertheless, the painting itself is a solid structure, and the composition has been carefully thought out. Jongkind never used oils in the open air; rather, he made quick, accurate sketches of natural objects with pencil and water color. With an extraordinary visual memory which enabled him to retain his impressions, he transformed his outdoor sketches into oil paintings in his studio.

Painting outdoors, one of the innovations of the Impressionist landscape painters, began with *Claude Monet* (1840–1926). Many of Monet's most beautiful paintings were created in small villages by the Seine, such as Argenteuil, or along the coast of Brittany. Whereas Constable and Jongkind were interested primarily in the subject, Monet's concern was color alone. A color's relationship to the whole work interested him, and he had an extraordinarily sensitive eye for the endless nuances of color. His tones were faultless, and he claimed that the spectator could guess the hour of the day from his paintings.

Fig. 56—CLAUDE MONET: *Japanese Footbridge and Water Lily Pool.* 1899. Collection of Mrs. Albert D. Lasker, New York.

No doubt Monet was one-sided in his endeavor to suppress all feelings and all knowledge and to concentrate solely on the impressions which strike the eye. Cézanne expressed the opinion that "Monet is only an eye—but what an eye!" Indeed, never did a painter's eye capture the most subtle nuances of color quite so accurately. His landscapes appeal to us because of their freshness and summer brightness.

When Impressionism became more appreciated, Monet's fortunes improved, and he was able to buy a house with a large garden and water lily pond in Giverny, north of Paris. There, in the last years of his life, he created the great series of paintings, "Les Nymphéas" ("The Water Lilies"), in which the reflection of the sky, of sunsets, and of stormy clouds in the quiet surface of the water unite with the water lilies and the hanging willow branches to form a surprising play of colors.

Among his paintings of the garden and pond is the "Japanese Footbridge and Water Lily Pool" (Fig. 56). In this work Monet penetrated so deeply into the mystery of light that he approached the borderline of abstraction. The intense, penetrating light dissolves everything and the composition consists of a pattern of color spots over the canvas.

Edouard Manet (1832–1883) is no doubt the outstanding talent of the whole movement. Less of a doctrinaire than Monet, he did not specialize in pure landscape. To him the views which were significant were the ones which captured Parisian life. His portraits and still lifes are works of rare beauty. In contrast to Monet, he retained a link with the old masters; in him one finds reminiscences of Velázquez, Hals, and Goya. The first paintings by Manet, "Le Déjeuner sur l'Herbe" (Fig. 57) and the nude "Olympia," introduced the new art form and created a scandal. Both of these works were indebted to Giorgione, Raphael, and Titian for their motifs and composition. What was new and shocking to the general public was the contemporary setting, the individual and wholly unidealized nude female figures, and the frank, unabashed look with which these figures engaged their viewers. Having been for so long protected by the saccharine, banal works produced and encouraged by the official Salon, the public was ill-prepared to find itself confronted in "Le Déjeuner

Fig. 57—Edouard Manet: *Le Déjeuner sur l'Herbe.* 1863. Louvre, Paris. (Archives Photographiques, Paris)

sur l'Herbe" by a Parisian prostitute, one of a group of Parisian picnickers, sitting on the grass in the foreground quite nude. This was an outrage to decency. The officials of the Salon were even more outraged by the painter's technique.

What defied the established rules and precepts in the nude "Olympia" was the way Manet allowed the figure to dominate the canvas, the way he used broad planes of flat colors and strong light tones against the dark hues—in other words, the way he delineated forms. In choosing to paint honestly rather than prettily, Manet stepped outside the Salon tradition, and the furor caused by his paintings provided a rallying point for other like-minded and equally revolutionary artists.

Manet usually worked in his studio, but he produced "The Painting Barge" (Fig. 58), a work dating from the early years of Impressionism, in the open air on the Seine. This work is his manifesto of "plein-air" painting and not only because of its subject—Claude Monet working in his floating studio, with his wife Camille. In this painting clear bright colors, which capture

Fig. 58—EDOUARD MANET: *The Painting Barge*. 1874. Alte Pinakothek, Munich.

the vibrant play of reflections on the water, and the broad strokes, which define the boat, give the illusion of sunshine and space. The solid shapes are not broken by floating particles of color, as with Monet. The composition, in horizontals and verticals, is more severe and the color contrasts stronger. Bright blues, yellows, greens, and whites are intensified by the black hull of the boat, on which the water casts blue and green reflections. Black, rejected by Monet as color but not as shadow, has been used by Manet to accent the sparkling color.

Auguste Renoir (1841–1919) expressed the joy of life and youth in his sunny landscapes and paintings of Parisian life, young women, and children. In the beginning he worked with Monet, Sisley, and Pissarro in the open air but later returned to the studio, where he could concentrate better. Renoir's way of indicating light and color differed from Monet's. With Renoir, capturing the eternal sunlight, not the fleeting moment, is important.

Fig. 59—AUGUSTE RENOIR: *Judgment of Paris. Ca.* 1914. Philadelphia Museum of Art, Philadelphia. (Collection of Henry P. McIlhenny)

His nudes—those, for instance, in his "Judgment of Paris" (Fig. 59)—are bathed in sunlight and are placed in a natural setting, although they were actually painted indoors. They are never erotic but have the natural innocence of healthy young animals and seem to belong to their surroundings. Renoir's adoration of Woman is best expressed in his paintings of robust, simple kitchen maids.

Edgar Degas (1834–1917) remained generally outside the main stream of Impressionism. Even less interested in the landscape than Manet, he used impressionistic techniques to create the illusion of motion. In the 1870's he found his motifs at the race course and depicted, for the first time, the horse in his natural gallop, as the camera first recorded it in photographs taken by Edward Muybridge in 1878. Previously, artists had depicted horses galloping with both fore- and hindlegs stretched out off the ground—a completely impossible position.

Fig. 60.—EDGAR DEGAS: *Dancers: Pink and Green.* 1890. Metropolitan Museum of Art, New York. (The Metropolitan Museum of Art, Bequest of Mrs. H. O. Havemeyer, 1929. The H. O. Havemeyer Collection)

Later, Degas discovered the world with which he is still associated: that of the dancing schools and the ballet. He often worked with pastels in order to reproduce better the delicate hues of gauze skirts and softly gleaming skin. His airy color, his retention of fleeting moment and enjoyment of the beauty of bodily movement support the position that he actually belonged to the Impressionists. But in other ways he stands apart from them. His compositions are carefully composed and have a solid structure. He was not only a sublime colorist as were the Impressionists, but a great draftsman as well, and he deeply respected the Neoclassicist Ingres. In addition, Degas was more than an "eye"; his paintings are psychological studies which reveal a rather cynical view of the world. In the dressing rooms and on the rehearsal stage, he saw the awkward forms and movements of the young girls and portrayed them with critical realism—as in "Dancers: Pink and Green" (Fig. 60).

Henri de Toulouse-Lautrec (1864–1901) was even further removed from Impressionism. His world was much different from that of Renoir and Degas, and his women were of another sort—the faded flower of the big town, the prostitute, and the cancan dancer.

Lautrec, a descendant of an old French family, broke both legs when he was a child and grew up to be an invalid dwarf. Possibly it was this physical handicap that made him a cynic and an alcoholic who moved in the shady world of Bohemian Paris, whose decadence he showed with merciless sincerity. Lautrec did not accuse like Daumier, nor did he take a secret pleasure in vice; rather, he presented these things as they were. He portrayed the low, the perverse, and the decadent of the *fin-de-siècle* with extraordinary insight.

The harmony between the subject and its treatment are evidence of Lautrec's great artistry. His preference for bold composition, powerful line, and strong color contrasts were ideally suited to the art form of his day: posters produced by lithography. The posters which Lautrec designed for such Paris cafés as the Moulin Rouge shocked the sensibilities of conservative society; they confronted the public with a lively art and caused one critic to remark, "The museum has moved to the streets. . ." The impact of Lautrec's art extended beyond his time to our own, and he is the spiritual father of a special type of art: modern poster painting.

Lautrec's art was influenced by Japanese prints—colored woodcuts which became widely known in Europe at that time. Manet, Degas, Lautrec, and Van Gogh greatly admired the art of Harunobu, Utamaro, and others. They were attracted not only by the subjects—the landscape and the life of the people—but also by the surprising composition and the color. These cuts, called *ukiyo-e,* meaning "flowing life," influenced line, color, and composition in both Degas and Lautrec.

The first current in art after Impressionism, called Neo-Impressionism, had few followers and soon reached a dead end. The Impressionists had maintained that all the hues of nature could be reproduced from the colors of the spectrum if these colors were distributed on the canvas unmixed and in little touches, and if it was left to the eye of the spectator to fuse them together. This system (called divisionism) was not used systematically by all Impressionists, some of whom also worked with transitional color hues. Neo-Impressionists applied color more scientifically than did the Impressionists. They systemized the distribution of color according to a rather complicated theory, taking the local colors into account—the warm hues (orange and yellow) added by the light, and the cool ones (green, blue, and violet) added by the shadows. Using unmixed colors applied to the canvas in little dots (a technique called pointillism), they produced a painting giving the desired effect only from a distance. Thus, the painter hoped to achieved a maximum of luminosity.

The most talented Neo-Impressionist was *Georges Seurat* (1859–1891). In his "Le Chahut" (Fig. 61) Seurat has shown the cancan, the dance performed in the cabarets of Montmartre and often painted by Toulouse-Lautrec. Two men and two girls, accompanied by an orchestra and surrounded by spectators, appear in the glare of artificial light. The numerous purple, blue, and pink dots impart a strange iridescent effect. Unlike an Impressionist painting, this work is not spontaneous but was produced laboriously, dot by dot. The methodical precision with which it was done is evident not only in the technique but also in the composition. This stark stylization leads to a monumentality which is alien to Impressionism.

In "Le Chahut" the parallel diagonals and counterdiagonals of the dancers' legs and the extremely long necks express the rhythm of the dance. In the expressionless faces and the artificial surroundings, something of the decadent, sensual, *fin-de-siècle* atmosphere is captured, revealing Seurat's own humane sensitivity. By his strict adherence to self-imposed rules, Seurat created an art which by its intense formulation approaches decoration. Yet reality, by virtue of this very formulization, is so crystallized in Seurat's works that they carry an undeniable authority and timelessness.

The pointillism of Seurat and *Paul Signac* (1863–1935) found followers in Belgium and Holland. Vincent van Gogh tried the technique during his Paris days, but this means of expression which required much patience, did not suit him, and he soon ended it. Nevertheless, Seurat's stylization, simplification, and severe organization, made later Cubists feel akin to him.

Fig. 61—GEORGES SEURAT: *Le Chahut*. 1889–90. Kröller-Müller Museum, Otterlo, Holland.

17

Post-Impressionism

(1880–1905)

The tendency in realistic seventeenth-century painting to reproduce the subject as faithfully as possible culminated, after a long evolution, in Impressionism, which in its pure form sought to record only sensory impressions of the outer world and ignored human values. Impressionists such as Degas and Toulouse-Lautrec, however, preferred to portray human situations rather than the landscape, and introduced psychological and social elements into their work. To them the artist had another function besides that of being only an "eye." But Impressionism, especially in Monet's work, disregarded two important aspects of the art of painting which had been greatly valued. It ignored, first of all, the spiritual content, which was of supreme importance for artists of the Middle Ages and the Renaissance. In the pursuit of constantly changing and form-dissolving light, it neglected also the pictorial structure, the composition.

After 1880 younger artists, called Post-Impressionists, began to feel that art had a socially-directed task and that it should be more highly organized and structured. At this time we also find a revival of interest in monumental wall painting and in stained glass, for in these were seen the ideal media for controlled composition and expressiveness. We can identify two main overlapping groups of Post-Impressionists. The first group objected to the lack of structure and solid form in Impressionism. Its leader was the great French painter Paul Cézanne, and his principles were the starting point for later Cubism and Nonobjective art.

The second group took issue with the lack of spiritual content. The master of this movement, which led to Expressionism, was Vincent van Gogh. These two, Cézanne and Van Gogh, along with the French painter Paul Gauguin (whose work influenced the Symbolist School and Art Nouveau), stand at the threshold of twentieth-century art. Thus we turn our attention to these painters and movements which ushered in modern art.

Paul Cézanne (1839–1906), one of the greatest masters of modern times, was the forerunner of Cubism. Cézanne lived the life of an ordinary Frenchman in the town of Aix-en-Provence. Although he had friends among the Impressionists, he did not belong to this group. His clear colors, however, remind us of their work. Like the Impressionists, Cézanne did not put an "idea" into his work; his starting point was *exclusively* visual, and he was interested, above all, in color. He did not want to capture momentary or fleeting impressions, but to create a solid and durable image. He was thinking of the kind of structure which Poussin's paintings had, and he turned to nature for his subjects—a reinterpretation of Impressionism with a formal and structural basis.

At first glance Cézanne's "Le Pont de Maincy" (Fig. 62) is little different from Monet's "Japanese Footbridge." But Monet dissolved all solid forms in the light, whereas Cézanne created them by organizing the structure in planes of color, a symphony of harmonious greens. Monet painted hastily to catch the fleeting effects of the light; Cézanne painted slowly and meticulously. Once Cézanne discovered the basic forms within the color complexes, he simplified them. The arches of the trees and the bridge, the verticals, horizontals, and diagonals are accentuated, giving the composition a concentration and compactness totally unlike the airy visions of the Impressionists. Cézanne did not use contours or perspective lines; his planes of color do not always touch and parts of the canvas are bare. The tension between these adjacent planes expresses spontaneously form, volume, and distance—in other words, perspective and space.

Cézanne's search for concentration of form within nature led him to the idea that all natural forms could be reduced to the basic cylinder, the sphere, and the cone. These basic shapes were not used as rigorously as they were by the later Cubists, but the geometrical forms can be clearly seen with Cézanne. A painting

Fig. 62—PAUL CÉZANNE: *Le Pont de Maincy. Ca.* 1885. Louvre, Paris. (Photo: Chuzeville)

by Cézanne often gives an abstract, almost stiff, impression, as if the subject has been crystallized. When Cézanne painted a portrait, he did so as if he were painting a basket of apples, searching out the architectonic relationships among the basic forms. Since he was not interested in the spiritual content, it seems only natural that he would be drawn toward the still life. Yet, here he was not interested in the *trompe l'oeil* ("almost real") effect achieved by the Dutch still-life painters of the seventeenth century and Courbet. His concern was with structure and form, and he used plaster fruits and paper flowers because real ones rotted and faded while he slowly worked out his techniques. Whatever he was painting Cézanne did not want to "model" but to "modulate"; he wanted to fill his canvas with harmonious planes of gleaming colors.

No contrast seems greater than that between Cézanne, who banished all spiritual content, and another great forerunner of modern art, *Vincent van Gogh* (1853–1890), whose art was a means of testifying to what moved his soul. There is something both artists have in common: the quest for that which is simple and fundamental. Cézanne looked for basic shapes; Van Gogh sought for an understandable, elementary symbolism. For Van Gogh inner perceptions and emotional experiences were transformed into changed and consistent forms; in this way his art reminds us of the art of the Middle Ages, which conveyed spiritual truths through familiar symbols. His forms and especially his color served to express an idea or a mood, not to reproduce visual reality. In this, his art anticipated Expressionism.

In his Dutch days, from 1881 until the end of 1885, Van Gogh used dark colors in his paintings of peasant life. He admired, above all, Millet and Josef Israels, painters who, like Daumier, evidenced strong sympathy with humanity. But Van Gogh's peasants are portrayed with even more intense compassion because of their despair-filled existence. There is no trace of idealization or sentimentality. "The Potato Eaters" (Fig. 63) stands out as a fine example of Van Gogh's early work. The peasant meal in this scene is painted in dismal colors, which reflect the wretched life of the family. The faces of the men are dulled by hard work. The shabby room of the hovel in which these people live is dimly lighted by an oil lamp. With grim penetration, Van Gogh's painting captures the essence of the fate of the poor Brabant peasants. Van Gogh was occupied at the time with naturalistic novels by Émile Zola, *Germinal* and *La Terre,* and something of Zola's brutal realism can be seen in "The Potato Eaters." No effort has been made to create a "beautiful" painting. "I would rather be myself," Van Gogh wrote, "and with rough execution say severe and harsh but true things." He wanted to show "that those hands which dip in the dish have worked in the earth itself, have done manual labor, and that they have thus earned their meal honestly."

Later in Paris, with his brother Théo, Van Gogh encountered French Impressionism, and soon afterward the dark, earthly colors vanished from his palette and gave way to bright plein-air hues. He learned the laws of color and painted with a divisionist technique; yet he did not become an Impressionist, for to him the visible world the sole concern of the Impressionists—was merely a symbol for the invisible one.

Fig. 63—VINCENT VAN GOGH: *The Potato Eaters*. 1885. Stedelijk Museum, Amsterdam. (Collection V. W. van Gogh)

In the early spring of 1888 Van Gogh went to Arles in southern France. There his vision changed and his work became a paean to the glory of nature. He called this time *le rayon ou la bonté* ("the radiant life") as opposed to *le rayon noir,* the darkness of his Brabant days. In gay light colors he painted trees and orchards in bloom. But the trees were neither impressions of color nor stones in the building of a composition. Because of their accented contours, the trees appear to leap from the earth—testimony to the creative energy and rejuvenating powers of nature. Symbolic meaning lies in everything; still, Van Gogh borrowed his symbols not from fantasy but from visual reality. A painting of a farmer sowing his crop hints at the spiritual link between man and the universe. Charged rhythmic brushstrokes unite the sky and the plow-combed field. The sun, under which the seeds will bud and the corn ripen, looms large and dominating—an ebullient source of life-giving power. For Van Gogh, "nature, clods of earth, yellow corn, peasants, were not only symbols of work, but also sources of consolation and strength."

Van Gogh did not hold to the Impressionist doctrine of "art for art's sake." To him it was the duty of art to *console* humanity. In this regard there is no clearer example than the painting called "La Berceuse," a portrait of Madame Roulin, wife of his friend the postman. Concerning the origin of this work, he explained that one day he and Gauguin (who visited him for a short time in Arles) were discussing the fishermen who had to make long voyages to Iceland. They talked about their loneliness on the inhospitable sea, and the thought came to Van Gogh to do such a painting as "La Berceuse" in order to give those sailors, who were at the same time children and martyrs, a feeling of rocking, something to remind them of lullabies from their youth. Van Gogh planned to hang the painting (actually he used the subject five times) in a sailor's café in Marseille, between two paintings with flaming yellow sunflowers which would illuminate it like two candles. The painting, he thought, should be one which the common sailor would be able to appreciate and should therefore have the character of a colored print from a bazaar: strong colors, mainly red and green, without many nuances, and simple form. Van Gogh's desperate melancholy and loneliness and the heartbreaking compassion he felt for the misery of others prompted

Fig. 64—VINCENT VAN GOGH: *Evening Landscape with Cypresses.* 1889–90. Kröller-Müller Museum, Otterlo, Holland.

him to paint as he did, and in "La Berceuse" he hoped to provide the thought of home for the simple souls at sea.

The works Van Gogh produced during his stay in the hospital of Saint-Rémy show clearly mental disorder resulting from his inner conflicts and suffering. In the "Evening Landscape with Cypresses" (Fig. 64), he saw the sun and moon not as sources of light but as heavenly bodies revolving in cosmic kinship with the earth. The strong color and violent movement express the tortured state of mind of its creator. Everything in this painting seems to flow—the cypress which resembles a flaming green torch, and the streamlike road with the little wagon and the two homeward-bound laborers. The creative process with Van Gogh was a means of release for his vision of a transformed world and a resolution of his own conflicts. Through his creativity, nature was indeed transformed, but it was because of the intensity of his soul and suffering.

A similar desire for simplification and symbolism is also found in the works of *Paul Gauguin* (1884–1903). For him, as with Van Gogh, encounter with corrupt modern society was too painful. He fled from the overcivilized and decadent atmosphere of Paris and sought new peace and nourishment for his art with people unspoiled by modern culture. Gauguin at first went to Brittany and painted the people of the village of Pont-Aven; later he traveled to the island of Tahiti in the South Pacific where he portrayed exotic scenes to which he gave Polynesian titles.

In one of these, "Nave Nave Mahana" (Fig. 65), the forms are flat patterns with no modeling; they are combined synthetically

Fig. 65—PAUL GAUGUIN: *Nave Nave Mahana*. 1896. Musée des Beaux-Arts, Lyons. (Photo: Camponogara)

in large planes separated from each other by heavy, dark contours and related through a strong rhythm. This is an art of decorative design and color—a new stylization, begun in 1888 by Gauguin in Pont-Aven, which derives from the technique of cloisonné enamel.

Gauguin wanted to paint the dreamlike happiness of people untouched by the quest for material gain, innocent and childlike people enjoying nature, which gives them everything they need and with which they are still closely linked. Because a process of thought was the basis of his art, Gauguin painted from memory, never directly from nature, as did Cézanne and Van Gogh. Gauguin departed even further from realistic representation than did Van Gogh. He painted violet trees and pink fields which combine to produce a perfectly natural, harmonious, and decorative effect. In contrast to Van Gogh, he spread his paint quite thin; thus, the rough texture of the canvas often shows through and reminds one of tapestries.

In addition to the great revolutionaries Cezanne, Van Gogh, and Gauguin, other painters appeared in the last years of the nineteenth century who turned away from Realism and Impressionism and drew from the "mysterious depths of thought."

The French painter *Odilon Redon* (1840–1916), who lived a withdrawn life near Bordeaux, wanted "to put the logic of the visible in the service of the invisible," and the way he painted all his subjects places them on the border between dream and reality: simple vases with flowers against a colorful background, heads of women, whose profiles remind one of paintings by Leonardo, or of strange apparitions from a fairy-tale world of poetic fantasy. He was repeatedly inspired by the thought of Pegasus, the winged horse of mythology. His rendition of form is often weak, but this is compensated for by the glowing unrealistic colors. In his lifetime more admired in other countries than in France, Redon is nowadays regarded as one of the forerunners of Surrealism.

Among the Paris Impressionists lived a painter whose art was of an altogether different world: *Henri Rousseau* (1844–1910). In order to distinguish him from three other painters with the same name—among them the Barbizon painter Théodore Rousseau—he was called "le Douanier" (the customs official), after his pro-

Fig. 66—Henri Rousseau: *The Sleeping Gypsy*. 1897. Museum of Modern Art, New York. (Collection, Museum of Modern Art, New York, Gift of Mrs. Simon Guggenheim)

fession. Rousseau worked at his art only on Sundays until his retirement in 1885, after which he devoted full time to his painting. He lacked professional training, but he had the simple faith, freshness, and naïveté of a child, and he stood completely outside the artistic schools of his day. His primitivism was imitated by many other Sunday painters, but none of them reached his level.

Biographies of Rousseau report (but no proof is given) that during his youth he served with a French expeditionary corps in Mexico. Perhaps reminiscences of the tropical jungle led him to create fantasies filled with the lush vegetation of exotic plants. At any rate, the artist has created a dreamland in which eyes of animals glitter through the leaves of trees, a snake charmer plays his flute, or a bright moon hangs in the sky.

"The Sleeping Gypsy" (Fig. 66) is permeated with a strange, unreal charm—the moonlit desert, the gypsy lying still as a wooden statue, her staff and musical instrument beside her, and the lion with the fascinating round eye and a mane which looks electrified. Another of his paintings, "The Dream," is a night scene in a jungle which shows large lotuslike flowers, tigers, an elephant, a pink snake, a flutist, and a naked girl lying on a couch. To an art critic's question about this work, Rousseau replied, "The woman dreams she is in the jungle listening to the flute."

The Belgian painter *James Ensor* (1869–1949), son of an English father and Belgian mother, began as an Impressionist with the technique of a virtuoso and a strong feeling for color; soon, however, he dropped the realistic subjects, still lifes, and interiors of his early days and fashioned his art into a game of original whims in which he showed his cynical view of life. He saw man as a grotesque, ridiculous being, and he exposed him as such—as, for instance, in his large painting "Entrance of Christ into Brussels" (now in the museum of Antwerp). His macabre fantasies full of masked carnival figures and skeletons depict the world as a play of marionettes. Man, seen as a being unable to control his own life and destiny, is reduced to a grinning mask and accompanied by the figure of Death.

Edvard Munch (1863–1944), the only painter from Norway of international importance, contributed greatly to the rise of Expressionism in Germany. "I do not paint what I see, but what I saw," Munch once said. Concerned with this inner vision, he has in common with Van Gogh a spiritual unrest; but he is more interested in the problems of the soul than in man's relation to nature. Sickness, life and death, obsessions, fear and despair are expressed in his wavy "brush writing," severely simplified forms, omission of details, and limited and intense colors. Expressions of despair and cries of fear echo in Munch's work—as in "The Scream."

The Swiss *Ferdinand Hodler* (1853–1918) also accentuated the rhythm of the line. Although he produced many Alpine landscapes, Hodler was in the first place a painter of figures. He built his compositions symmetrically, monumentally, and with strong contours—concentrating on large planes, strong symbolic colors, and symbolic images, which, as with Munch, suggest in their conception monumental wall painting.

Several Symbolist movements of the last decade of the nineteenth century stemmed directly from Paul Gauguin's art. The intention of the Symbolists was not to imitate nature but to express spiritual reality. They rejected perspective and the color analysis of the Impressionists. In the place of these they put "synthesis"—a concentration on broad, flat planes which tended toward decoration rather than illusionism.

In 1890 the art critic Albert Aurier wrote an article in the magazine *Mercure de France* in which he discussed the principles of Symbolism. To Aurier a work of art must evidence: (1) *idea,* because that is its purpose, (2) *symbolic intention,* because that is what gives the idea a certain form, (3) *synthesis,* because this gives these forms and signs a general summing up, (4) *subjectivity,* because what the artist sees in things matters, not the things themselves, and (5) *decorativeness,* as the logical consequence of the first four points.

In France, one group of Symbolists came together in Brittany, around Gauguin and his friend Émile Bernard, while a second group formed in Paris. Included in this latter group, called "Les Nabis" (a Hebrew word for "prophets"), were *Maurice Denis* (1870–1943), *Pierre Bonnard* (1867–1947), and *Edouard Vuillard* (1868–1940). The last two soon left the Symbolist movement and returned to the portrayal of external reality, such as interiors with figures, interpreting these intimate scenes in a poetic and decorative way and using very fine harmonies of color.

The decorative side of Symbolist art had no consistent characteristics because it manifested itself in many forms, but akin to it was a new movement which appeared in the 1890's. This style was variously termed *Jugendstil* in Germany and Austria, *Art Nouveau* in France, and *Modern Style* in England. The movement, characterized by an extensive stylization and rhythmic lines, is related to another *fin-de-siècle* phenomenon: Rococo. Like Rococo, Art Nouveau was especially used in architecture and applied arts—interior decorations, furniture, fashions, bric-à-brac, and ceramics. Most of its decorative motifs were flowers borrowed from plant life. Centers of this new art were to be found in Vienna, Munich, Barcelona, and Belgium. In Paris the style made its appearance in iron arabesques of the old gates to the subway.

Art Nouveau originated in the decorative lines of the paintings and woodcuts by Gauguin, in the wavy brush work of Van Gogh's last paintings, and in the elegant arabesques of Japanese woodcuts, which have had great influence on European painting since Impressionism. "Le Chahut" by Seurat, the "Evening Landscape with Cypresses" by Van Gogh, the posters by Toulouse-Lautrec, and the paintings by Edvard Munch and Ferdinand Hodler, all are enlivened by linear rhythms which were reflected for a long time afterward in the composition of Henri Matisse.

18

Currents in the Twentieth Century

Within the humanist tradition, man was the explorer of a world which, by investigation, could be clarified or rationally explained. From the Renaissance through the nineteenth century the faith in man's ability to understand the world around him was reflected in his art. The images he created were substantial reflections of the world he perceived. To this extent, the Renaissance tradition which culminated in nineteenth-century art may be said to be *physio-plastic,* that is, it began in the sensory perceptions of an understandable environment.

In the twentieth century, society was finally wrenched loose from its complacency. In one short decade discoveries by Planck, Einstein, and Freud had overthrown traditional views of matter and man (and in the process almost shattered both). The new theories of quantum physics, relativity, and psychoanalysis, among others, challenged all that once seemed so certain and so real to the senses. Man's understanding of his own significance and his belief that this is the "best of all possible worlds" had to be adjusted to new perspectives which included the infinitesimally small, the atom, and the immeasurably large, the universe, in which the earth is only a speck of dust. The discovery that reality existed beneath or beyond surface appearances destroyed the last vestiges of the artist's faith in the world of the senses. But it remained for him to give form and meaning to the reality which best represented the new view of the world, and to produce images of his newly acquired knowledge (or lack of it). The twentieth-century artist could no longer use traditional forms; instead, he developed new means of expression based on inner experience, on a collaboration of intellect and intuition, and these new forms we may call *ideo-plastic*. Despite the variety of expression among contemporary artists, however, there is one point they hold in common—their rejection of the reproduction of visual reality. This has led to a highly abstract art, sometimes disconcerting to a public accustomed to the forms used by the old masters. Nevertheless, the new world vision, in many ways a logical continuation of the old, finds its expression in modern art and provides an interpretation and clarification of the experience of our age.

Artists, in their search for means to express the contemporary view of man and his world, have developed four distinct approaches. As they will be summarized here, these approaches, or styles, within the modern movement move progressively further away from visual reality.

1. *Expressionism* springs from the internal wells of subjective experience and through intensification and symbolism expresses the irrational and emotional side of man's nature. The Expressionist painter changes (distorts) forms and colors. He simplifies them in order to make them more intense. The Fauves, who carried these distortions to the extreme, were forerunners of Expressionism. Earlier painters who used distortions were Grünewald and El Greco.
2. *Surrealism and Fantasy* touch the area of psychoanalysis and explore the world of dreams, free association, and poetic fantasy. The Surrealist artist explores the regions of man's subconscious impulses and feelings. The fantastic dream visions of Hieronymous Bosch are most akin to Surrealist art.
3. *Cubism* reorders the external world in terms of interrelated basic shapes. Originally, Cubist paintings were inspired by the formal logic of mathematics and the functional cohesion of machinery, and were produced by Picasso (the foremost exponent of the style), Braque, Gris, and Léger between 1907–14. The style was a continuation of Cézanne's simplification of color planes; however, modern Cubists go much further and reduce objects to simple shapes which they then survey from various points and reconstruct into a completely new structure in an artificially created space.

4. *Nonobjective Art* dispenses completely with any re-creation of recognizable objects in order that the pure relationships of form and color might be raised above finite identifications and might express universal truths. It is an art which seeks to approach the mysterious threshold of music and mathematics. In his book *Plastic Art and Pure Plastic Art* (1937), Piet Mondrian described the advent of abstraction as the moment in which the culture of particular form approaches its end and the culture of determined relations begins. Nonobjective art is based exclusively on a rhythmic or constructive division of the plane, on the relationship and tension between forms and colors. The first Nonobjective painting seems to be a water color by Wassily Kandinsky in the year 1910, for the past does not provide examples of purely Nonobjective art.

EXPRESSIONISM

In Paris around 1905, lived a group of painters called "Les Fauves" (wild beasts) because of their violent reaction against naturalistic representation of things; these painters followed the path of Van Gogh and Gauguin and must be recognized as the forerunners of Expressionism. The Fauves went further in the use of distortion than either Van Gogh or Gauguin, and their color was even further removed from reality. It is no wonder that the public, barely accustomed to Impressionism, was greatly shocked by their paintings.

Henri Matisse (1869–1954) was the leader of the group, which included, among others, Rouault, Utrillo, Marquet, Vlaminck, Dufy, and Van Dongen. Like Gauguin, Matisse sacrificed visual reality (or representation) for synthesis and simplification. In his paintings there is no perspective or illusion of space; the canvas is filled with decorative, playful arabesques enclosing even planes of color. Matisse used extremely thin paints which allowed rapid painting akin to the water-color technique. The effect is one of engaging spontaneity and ease, and the viewer is tempted to regard this art as childlike. We should not assume, however, that the work is actually spontaneous. Only after many preliminary sketches did the work acquire its final form. The purpose is to

Fig. 67—HENRI MATISSE: *The Purple Robe*. 1937. Baltimore Museum of Art, Baltimore. (Courtesy of The Baltimore Museum of Art, Cone Collection)

create a pleasing composition which has harmony and balance.

In the painting "The Purple Robe" (Fig. 67), the face of the woman is nothing more than an oval with lines for the eyebrows and dots for the eyes and mouth. This work has a real French airiness and charm, and the light, gay, intense colors express a happiness and an acceptance of life. "I dream," wrote the artist, "of an art of balance, purity, and serenity, an art devoid of depression or disquiet, but which has a calming influence on every mental worker, like a sweet consolation or an easy chair, in which one can rest after physical fatigue." Such a statement may help us to understand why Matisse neglected all details, such as facial features. If he had painted them, then he would have indeed created faces instead of, as he intended, spots of color playing their role in a magic carpet of colors. A decorator of genius, Matisse looked for expression in the joyous effect of color, line, and rhythm.

There are great differences between Matisse and *Georges Rouault* (1871–1958). For Rouault, art was a means of expressing his religious feelings. An artist of deep Christian conviction (a rarity in modern art), Rouault turned against middle-class hypocrisy and convention. His images are those of people who stand outside society. Again and again he painted clowns, who in their apparent self-inflicted ridiculousness are deeply tragic, and in that tragedy achieve a power of expression reminding us of Christ's suffering.

To understand Rouault's artistic form, one should know that he began as an apprentice to a stained-glass window maker and had great admiration for the medieval window with its deep color-glow, framed in heavy lead. We can still recognize these window elements in the wide, black contours within which Rouault applied his paint in relief, giving it the glowing fire of precious stones. His method seems primitive and his figures barbaric, but his rough indication of the face, nose, and eyes and the heavy strokes and intense color with the dark contours and shadow are done intentionally. A careful treatment would make the painting conventional and weaken the expression. How seriously Rouault considered his art was demonstrated in 1947 when he burned more than three hundred paintings because he was dissatisfied with them.

Expressionism gives form and color to inner experience while distorting natural color and form. At various times throughout the history of art, the qualities of Expressionism have been present in some way or other—in the medieval miniatures, with Grünewald, and with El Greco, to cite a few examples. As a

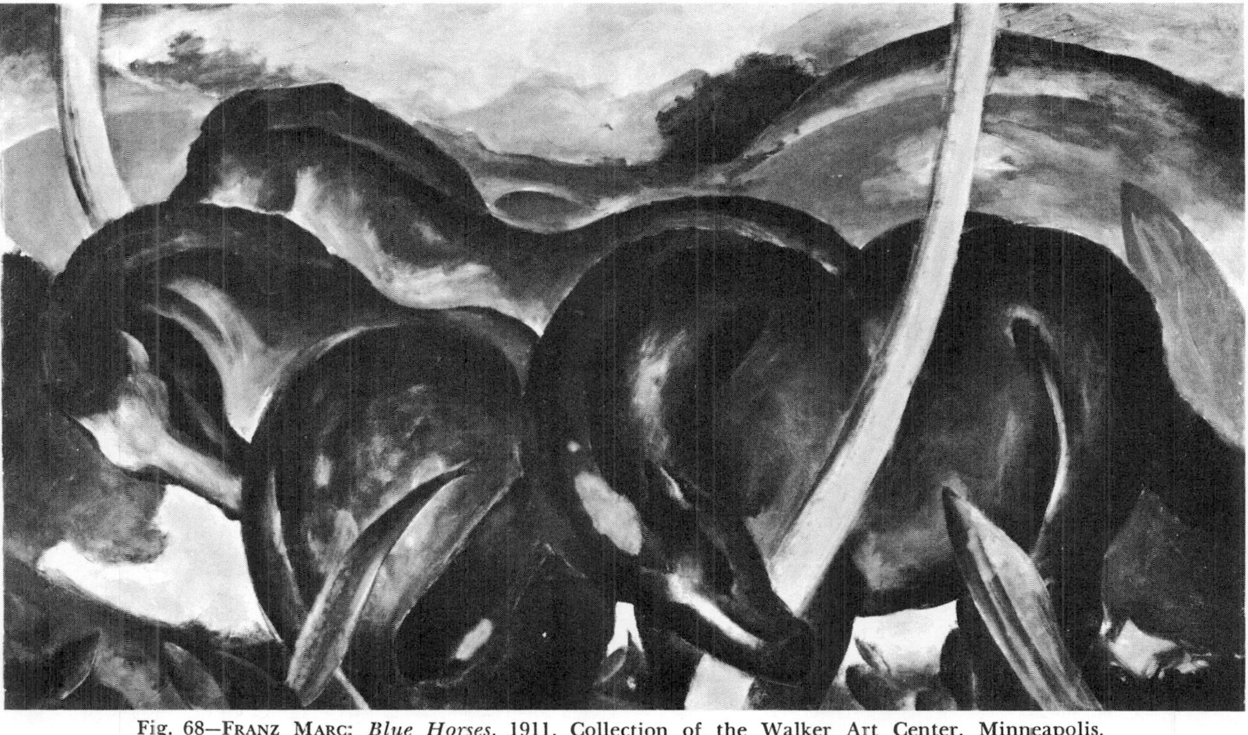

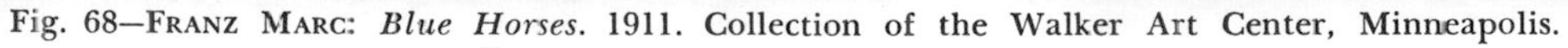

Fig. 68—FRANZ MARC: *Blue Horses*. 1911. Collection of the Walker Art Center, Minneapolis.

specific movement of painters of the twentieth century, however, German Expressionism originated in the nineteenth century through the influence of Vincent van Gogh, Ensor, Munch, and Hodler.

The first Expressionist group originated in 1905 in Dresden, Germany, around the same time the Fauves were shocking Paris. This group called itself "Die Brücke" (The Bridge), and among its members were Kirchner, Heckel, Nolde, and Pechstein. A second group formed in 1910 in Munich under the name "Der Blaue Reiter" (The Blue Rider), the title of a painting by Wassily Kandinsky, and also of a book published by him and his collaborator Franz Marc. Other members who carried the influence of the German Expressionists forward were the Swiss *Paul Klee* (1879–1940) whose influence is important in modern art, and *August Macke* (1887–1914) and *Franz Marc* (1880–1916), both of whom were killed in World War I.

Marc has become famous as a painter of animals, but his style is neither realistic nor impressionistic. He depicted the animal in unnatural colors but with a love for its wildness, its playfulness, and its unity with nature. In the painting "Blue Horses" (Fig. 68) the entire background is painted in fierce tones of orange, green, and purple. The blue forms of the horses are stylized and simplified to their essentials. Their curves and movements express mobility and sportiveness. In his later work Marc was influenced by Cubism and constructed his pictures in geometrical, crystallike shapes which approached the borderline of abstraction.

Other important representatives of Expressionism include *Paula Modersohn-Becker* (1876–1907), who worked in the artists colony of Worpswede on the Lüneburger moor in Germany; the Austrian *Oskar Kokoschka* (1886–); and *Max Beckmann* (1884–1950), who worked in Amsterdam from 1937 until 1947. In Belgium the most important Expressionist painter was *Constant Permeke* (1886–1952), who painted workers, farmers, and seamen in brown and ocher colors. In Holland, we also find elements of Expressionism in the works of *Jan Sluyters* (1881–1957), *Herman Kruyder* (1881–1935), and *Hendrik Chabot* (1894–1949).

SURREALISM AND FANTASY

Expressionism developed further into an art form which looked for subjects in the realm of fantasy and the dream world and the life of the subconscious (as investigated by Freud). The Surrealists liked to portray strangeness, oppression, and terror of the dream world. André Breton, the spokesman of Surrealism, declared in 1924 that Surrealism is a pure "psychic automatism, by which it is intended to express, whether verbally or in writing, or in any other way, the real process of thought. Thought's dictation, free from any control by the reason, independent of any esthetic or moral preoccupation." When control of the mind is eliminated (something that happens with normal human beings only during their dreams), the most absurd and illogical things take place. The Surrealist does not paint the dream vision itself but applies the dream process to depict grotesque situations and objects in an unreal relationship. Important to the Surrealist is the presentation of these unreal things in an extremely realistic and convincing way, in a smooth conventional style.

The most important figures of Surrealism are the Spaniards *Joan Miró* (1893–) and *Salvador Dali* (1904–), the German *Max Ernst* (1891–), and the Frenchman *Yves Tanguy* (1900–1955). In Belgium, Surrealism has been represented by *Paul Delvaux* (1897–) and *René Magritte* (1898–). In France, it found a very satisfactory medium of expression in the tapestry, which traditionally, much more than the painting, belongs in an atmosphere of dream and poetry.

The world of the imagination is portrayed by a number of artists not of the Surrealist school. The "Pittura Metafisica" (Metaphysical Picture) was introduced between 1910 and 1915 in Paris by an Italian of Greek origin, *Giorgio de Chirico* (1888–). In the present age of the machine De Chirico's concept of man is that of a puppet assembled from pieces of iron, nuts, and bolts. His puppets take their names from antiquity (as Hector and Andromache); in this way De Chirico expresses his nostalgia for the classical humanistic world. His paintings of city views are equally dehumanized. Open squares surrounded by palaces and colonnades are painted with great clarity in a gripping atmosphere under a steel-blue sky—a setting in which time and space are held in some strange suspension. Streets are deserted save for some senseless classical statues and long, threatening shadows, a clock, the silhouette of a train or factory in the distance beyond a wall. All are evocative as the titles of the paintings themselves:

Fig. 69—A. C. WILLINCK: *Simon the Stylite.* 1939. Municipal Museum, The Hague.

"The Soothsayer's Recompense," "Nostalgia of the Infinite," and "Place d'Italie." The world into which De Chirico leads us is petrified and lifeless, an empire of the dead.

After World War I, a current developed in Germany and also in Holland that reacted against the distortions of Expressionism and applied itself to an almost photographic reproduction—called "New Realism" and sometimes "Magic Realism" because of its unreality. In Holland the movement included among its followers *Pyke Koch* (1901–   ) and *A. C. Willinck* (1900–   ).

In Willinck's "Simon the Stylite" (Fig. 69) a man sits on one of the broken pillars of an ancient temple and looks toward the sky. In the background—a completely deserted and petrified landscape—we see a town in flames; dark smoke clouds drift over the land and blot out the sky. There is no logical connection between the man and his deserted surroundings or the burning town. In this clear, photographically sharp picture of reality, the painter has evoked a strange, unreal image of a doomed world.

Fig. 70—MARC CHAGALL: *Cellist*. 1939. Stedelijk Museum, Amsterdam.

The strong dream element in the work of *Marc Chagall* (1887–) makes him also akin to the Surrealists. Chagall was born into a poor Russian Jewish family but spent most of his life in France. The impressions from his early youth—the little houses in his village of birth, the synagogue, the moon above the snowy roofs, his father selling herring, an uncle playing the violin—all have remained dominant in his emotional life and art. Repeatedly one finds these elements combined to express the content of his childhood and inner experience which have been transformed and relived in a fairylike, unreal atmosphere.

In his "Cellist" (Fig. 70) Chagall shows the musician who has become one with his instrument, and who rises on the wings of the spirit. Towering above the low houses of a Russian village at night, his waving hair blending with currents of air, he penetrates a rhythmic sky sown with flowering branches. Alongside this higher manifestation of man freed of earthly ties sits his powerless lower self, small and miserable and bound to the earth, symbolized by a goat man. The cellist's face, painted in profile and from the front (the simultaneous reproduction also found with Picasso and in general the Cubists), gives an impression of movement. Throughout, Chagall's works breathe a warm feeling for mankind—something which cannot be said to belong to the Surrealists.

PICASSO AND CUBISM

The large Cézanne exhibition of 1907 and the discovery of the expressive force of Negro sculpture gave impetus to a new movement—called "Cubism"—which has played one of the most important roles in modern art. Cubism was first formulated around 1908 by Picasso and Braque, who arrived at the completely new method of expression in their efforts to free the painter entirely from nature.

Pablo Picasso (1881–), the most difficult-to-classify, most discussed twentieth-century artist, was led by his restless spirit and wide-ranging imagination to explore and to create a multitude of styles in which the modern period may see its reflection. In his Expressionist period (the "blue period" of 1901–04, followed by a "pink period" of 1904–07) he painted people who stood outside middle-class society—acrobats, harlequins, rope dancers, the poor, the lonely, and the outcast. Even in these early works we find a tendency toward abstraction, but it is hidden in the antisociality of his people, their gaudy costumes, the bareness of the setting in which they move. These paintings are still connected with the humanist tradition that Picasso was soon to abandon in favor of Cubism. Picasso, however, has never stood completely still. Although the development of Cubism is one of his finest achievements, he has gone beyond this in other experiments. In 1937, for instance, he relied on all his early Cubist techniques and experience in creating a masterwork—the "Guer-

Fig. 71—PABLO PICASSO: *Guernica*. 1937. Museum of Modern Art, New York. (On extended loan to the Museum of Modern Art, New York, from the artist)

nica" (Fig. 71) which demonstrates, in a way akin to Goya, the terror and helplessness that is a consequence of the violence of war.

The term "Cubism," allegedly coined by the same critic who first used the name "Fauves," is obviously not appropriate. The structure of the plane has nothing to do with cubes, for the forms are strongly distorted geometrically. What the Cubists did was to create an abstract * art; they restructured visual reality to a degree which, when it was expressed within the painting, no longer pointed to the reality outside itself, but created a new reality. In doing this, the Cubists were freeing art from a dependence upon nature, realizing more fully than any of the preceding masters the inherent independence of the painting, that is to say, its abstract nature.

Cubism ended the role of painting as "a window opening onto nature." The Cubist did not see things in the form of their optical appearance, or from one point of view. Just as important to an understanding of the essence of things is what cannot be seen. Thus, the Cubist looked at his subject from several sides, dissecting it into its components and building out of those several aspects a new composition of his own making. The artist was led not by the eye but by the brain; his interest now was in constructing, not imitating. With Cubism, painting assumed a new role, an autonomous, independent role, no longer an imitation of something outside itself (nature) but capable of making statements in its own terms.

The first stage, in which the object falls apart in stereometrical forms which penetrate each other, was called "Analytical Cubism" (1909–12). Form was the main preoccupation and color was only an accompaniment, mainly restricted to nuances of gray and brown. With these experiments, Braque and Picasso confined themselves mainly to still lifes of suitable objects: fruit, bowls,

* It is true that all painting, and sculpture, is abstract in that it is a representation of something else. A painting of a tree, for instance, is not the tree itself. The *degree* to which the depiction captures or departs from the appearance of the object depicted determines the degree of abstraction. Thus, many works and styles may be termed more "abstract" than others, even within the representational tradition. El Greco and Grünewald used distortion for expressive purposes, whereas Piero della Francesca and Poussin exaggerated the qualities of structure and clarity to achieve rationality and balance.

Fig. 72—GEORGES BRAQUE: *Still Life*. 1928. Stedelijk Museum, Amsterdam.

bottles, glasses, musical instruments—that is to say, things which already have a geometrical form.

The second phase, called "Synthetic Cubism," was formulated between 1912 and 1914. Here, the crystallike parts float together forming larger planes and recognition becomes easier. Color began to play an increasingly larger role and compositions of great charm were created. Sometimes, other materials—such as pieces of paper, wood, and sand—were incorporated into the painting surface. An example of "Synthetic Cubism" is the "Still Life" (Fig. 72) by *Georges Braque* (1882–). The objects here are presented on a sort of flat surface, not as they actually appear in the real world, but as they pass through the mind's eye, as impressions. The light parts are emphasized and framed by the planes of darker color. In this kind of painting we can admire the color as a whole, the divisions of light and dark, and the strong composition.

Two Cubist painters who also made important contributions must be mentioned: *Juan Gris* (1887–1927), a Spanish artist who worked in France, and *Fernand Léger* (1881–1955). Gris followed a preconceived design on which the forms were imposed—a technique which did much to further the autonomy of the work of art. Léger developed a very personal style, inspired by the machine. In it, he expresses the spirit of our mechanized time. He built his figures out of elements which remind us of cogwheels, flywheels, and especially tubes (which have given him the nickname "le Tubiste"). Léger's compositions, particularly the later ones, are simple and clear in intent; the colors are uncomplicated and confined to the primary ones, which often stand out against a white background.

NONOBJECTIVE ART

Cubism represented one road away from traditional representational painting. It went far in its realization of the abstract qualities of a work of art. Although it still borrowed its motifs from the visible world, it transformed them into a new reality, dissociated from nature and rendered in a new form, a geometric pattern and a color composition which had nothing to do with local color and the depiction of objects, but which was based, rather, on the beauty of the material of painting itself. Another and perhaps more daring road was that of Nonobjective painting. In this, the degree of abstraction is complete. It is not in any way visual re-creation of objective reality and it has no point of departure in familiar objects. It begins and ends with the medium itself, and its poetry and impact is that which form and color alone may evoke.

The first Nonobjective movement, Russian in origin, began with *Wassily Kandinsky* (1866–1945), who in 1910 painted the first completely abstract work, a water color which he called "Dots of Color Creating Feeling." It has been said that Kandinsky came to his art in the following way. Once, when he entered his studio at twilight, he saw one of his paintings with a definite subject in bright colors, standing upside down against a wall. The subject was unrecognizable; yet, he was struck by the beauty of the painting and decided to experiment with nonrepresentational painting. In his later work, such as "Entre Deux" (Fig. 73), Kandinsky created free, seemingly imaginary forms, which, however, remind us of the basic forms of nature,

Fig. 73—Wassily Kandinsky: *Entre Deux*. 1934. Collection Pierre Peissi, Paris.

of lower organisms such as bacteria. This art can fascinate us through its playfulness and fantasy and through the extremely refined play of color.

A few years after Kandinsky's first experiment, his compatriot *Kasimir Malevich* (1878–1935) arrived at an abstract art very different from Kandinsky's rhythmic, decorative, and "romantic" concept. In 1913 Malevich exhibited in Moscow a painting which showed nothing but a black square on a white background. "This square," said Malevich, "is not without content, because it ex-

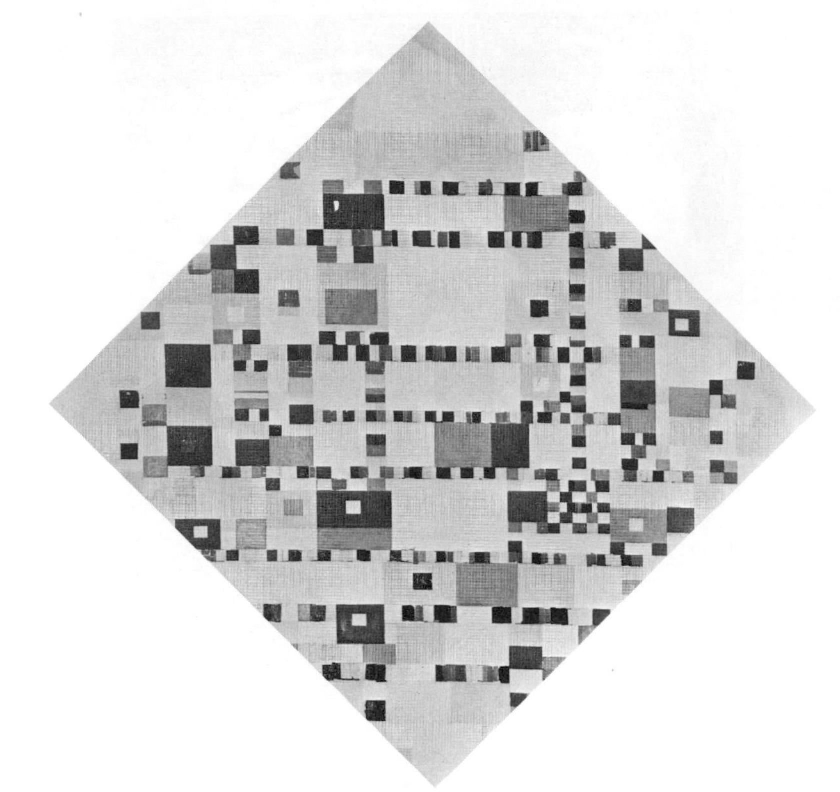

Fig. 74—Piet Mondrian: *Victory Boogie Woogie*. 1943–44. Museum of Modern Art, New York. (On extended loan to the Museum of Modern Art, New York, from Mr. and Mrs. Burton Tremaine)

presses the absence of an object." From then on, he confined his paintings to colored squares and triangles, circles, and trapeziums. With these elementary geometric forms he tried to create an impression of vastness, infinity, and supernaturalness. Because all details are suppressed, Malevich called his art "Suprematism." He achieved the purest form in a painting when he exhibited in 1919 in Moscow a work showing a white square on a white background.

The contrast between these two Russian artists is evidence that even in its beginning Nonobjective art was divided into two currents—a dynamic one based on feeling, and a constructive one. Belonging to the latter current is one of the earliest and most important abstract movements, called "De Stijl" (after a magazine of that name originated by its leader, Theo van Doesburg), which was formed in 1917 by a group of Dutch painters and architects.

The most important representative of "De Stijl," *Piet Mondrian* (1872–1944), evolved a style which he called "Neo-Plasticism" and which was based on a balanced division of the plane by horizontal and vertical lines, enclosing squares of even colors. The color, as pure as the composition, is confined to the primaries–red, yellow, and blue–with the addition of black, white, and gray. In his last works, created in New York, black has disappeared, and a lively rhythm has been introduced through smaller planes of color, as in "Victory Boogie Woogie" (Fig. 74). This is an art of balance and tension, in which the artist has freed himself in order that, in Mondrian's words, "The versatility of Nature can be reduced to the plastic expression of definite relations." His experiments, premised on the idea that painting is similar to architecture in its construction, depends on the arrangement of forms and colors for its effect.

19

The Role of American Painting

by Professor John Sedgwick

Although the great American art was that of the pre-Columbian cultures of Peru and Mexico, there is also a formidable and promising art of the North American continent, an offshoot of the European tradition, but with forms and motivations of its own. Among these latter American arts, painting is by no means the least.

American painting (by which we mean the painting of the colonies and the United States) * does not differ from French painting as does, say, English or Spanish painting. America is not a country but a civilization, and its art differs from that of Europe not simply in matters of national temperament, but rather as to the *kind of art* involved.

American art has generally been motivated by the prosaic rather than the poetic. This does not mean that America can not produce great poets in paint, such as Albert Ryder and Franz Kline, but that the American attitude toward art is not in the European tradition of the aesthetic, as centering around the "beautiful object." American art seeks its highest values in truth and action. There is, therefore, a continuity in motivation from the earliest "limners" (anonymous backwoods portrait painters)

* It should be observed before passing that modern Mexico also has famous art production. Painters such as José Orozco (the best), Diego Rivera, David Siqueiros, and Rufino Tamayo are certainly deserving of attention, but in the end their art seems too programmatic and, while sincere, still too obviously motivated to find resolution in terms of a vital style. With the best intentions art can never be manufactured, and one might conclude that, if their cause was just, their art was just fair.

to Copley in the eighteenth century, to Ryder and Eakins in the nineteenth, and to Pollock and De Kooning in the twentieth.

Such an evolution, which is not nearly so consistent nor persistent as that of any major European painting tradition, nevertheless also shows an emphasis on certain commensurate qualities, such as directness, clarity, simplicity, even naïveté, and the frequent emergence of that which is vigorous, functional, and cantankerously independent. These quantities to be sure are equally marked in distinguishing American politics or society from that of the home countries.

As in social history, the home countries play a decreasingly significant role in the formation of American painting. In the seventeenth and eighteenth centuries the influence of the Dutch and English schools was paramount (and attributable to the fact that such large proportions of colonists derived from those countries). In the nineteenth century the accession to influence of the French school was, however, primarily attributable to its dominance in the European painting of its day, and it was then that for the first time American artists responded consciously to the contemporary European traditions.

In the twentieth century the European influences on American painting became increasingly international until, in the 1940's, the weight of creativity and leadership in painting passed noticeably from the European continent to the American. Today, American painters (who were not all born or even trained in this country) stand at the center of the world's interest and influence.

There is no space here for a survey of the development of American painting over more than two important centuries, and we must be content to consider certain Americans who belong permanently in the history of Western painting—who have made, so to speak, the world scene.

The first American painter of absolute rank was *John Singleton Copley* (1738–1815). From a rather meagre knowledge of European painting derived chiefly through engravings and replicas, Copley produced portraits equal to any of his generation anywhere. On the eve of the Revolution, when he was at the height of his matured powers, he moved to England; there, for the rest of his life, he painted pictures increasingly cognizant of technical facility and increasingly devoid of creative force and definition. His is one of the supreme tragedies in American painting, though not the only one of its kind, for other American artists—even until the early twentieth century—were to be overcome by the accumulated glory of European painting and were to surrender thereto their native powers of naïve focus and primitive directness that alone could make possible a vital and meaningful American art form.

One of the most penetrating of portraitists, Copley in his prime could find and express in his paintings qualities and experiences in his sitters that they knew not themselves—until they and their friends saw them upon the canvas. But it is not psychological vision only that makes a work of art in portrait painting, and Copley gave forms to these experiences that oblige us to see him as a creative composer.

The simplicity of many of his single portraits is deceptive, for their evocation of the isolation of the individual in that hard new environment, and of the strength of will of his control over it and over himself, is a subtle product of precise adjustments and definitions. In a group portrait such as that of "Governor and Mrs. Thomas Mifflin" (Fig. 75), the mastery of Copley's composing is perhaps more evident.

The extraordinary fusion of the sense of self-sufficient independence of the individual apart, and the eloquent development of a play of responses between the two (so that we know they must be intimately related and know further something of the social and individual values of that relationship), are inseparable from the amazing inventiveness of gesture and pictorial accent. In the manipulation of cords, books, fingers, and furniture, not only painting but an entire society was being "fashioned" with that incomparable dexterity and decision that was soon to be seen in the polity of the founding fathers and is seen already here in the pictorial prophecy of a founding father of American art.

As always, at least until the mid-twentieth century, it is difficult to compare for final quality the work of American and European painters. If supreme among American painters of the eighteenth century, how does Copley stand in comparison with his European contemporaries? Surely we cannot consider him a titan of

Fig. 75—JOHN SINGLETON COPLEY: Governor and Mrs. Thomas Mifflin. 1773.
From the Collection of the Historical Society of Pennsylvania.

the world's art alongside Goya; yet Copley's best portraiture is in certain ways superior to Goya's and that is no mean thing. Similarly, while lacking Gainsborough's grace and range, Copley nevertheless produced single works as impressive as almost any of that fine English master's.

Copley is important for the American tradition in another way: along with Benjamin West (actually a bad painter, but significant as a fine teacher and as an American who became head of the British Royal Academy), Copley developed conceptions of the historical picture ahead of those European painters who were to make of it one of the major developments of the first part of the nineteenth century. (By historical picture here is meant the rendering of a significant event on an imposing scale, an event close enough in both time and space to painter and spectator to be of contemporary issue.) Pictures such as West's painting of "Penn's Treaty with the Indians," or the "Death of General Wolfe," and Copley's "The Death of Chatham," "The Death of Major Pierson," or the vast "Repulse of the Floating Batteries at Gibralter" set the stage for Goya's war pictures and prints, and for the elaborated reportage of David, Delacroix, or Géricault. Indeed, the latter's monumental "Raft of the Medusa" is so close in concept and composition to another historical picture of Copley's, "Brook Watson and the Shark," that it may well have been inspired thereby.

Thus, the inventiveness which we find stylistically in Copley's composition and expression is echoed historically in his concept of themes; and while the historical pictures are qualitatively by no means Copley's best (though containing splendid passages), this is not unusual. American art often has started things that others (especially the French, who are old hands at this sort of thing) were to carry to fuller and more finished conclusions. The role of innovator is a persistent one in American painting and takes a perhaps ironic but by no means insignificant turn in the careers of men such as Charles Willson Peale who partially, or Samuel F. B. Morse who entirely, forsook painting for the art of invention itself.

While the painting of seventeenth- and eighteenth-century America was almost exclusively portrait painting, that of the nineteenth century was dominated—though by no means so exclusively—by landscape. A stunning exception, and the last great portrait painter in America, was *Thomas Eakins* (1844–1916). His portrait subjects differ from Copley's in that they seem immersed in, rather than definitive of, their environment. (It is this immersion in nature that makes the nineteenth century generally a period of paramount landscape experience.) Eakin's style compared to Copley's is more "painterly" and less draftsmanlike, though Eakins too was a great draftsman in paint. This difference in style is attributable both to Eakins' personal expression and to the basic experience of his generation. One of the things that ruined Copley was the conscious attempt to make his style more painterly.

With Eakins this rich fabric and substance is always at the service of a strong will and temperament, and under the discipline of what amounted virtually to scientific investigations of such phenomena as the precise movement of a boat sailing through water, of a horse trotting, of a man rowing, or of a boxer's movement as an anatomist would know it. He developed a professional knowledge of these and other mathematical and scientific studies, such as the motion picture—of which he was a pioneer.

Such accomplishments do not make an artist, but they were symptomatic of Eakins' view that his art consisted of paddling his canoe in a course parallel to nature's—a concept of the function of art surprisingly similar to that of his French contemporary, Paul Cézanne, whose work or thought he could hardly have known. Out of the analytic vision and steely study that motivates his pictures of rowers and sailers, of horses and prizefighters, of the form of the female throat in song—as well as the contemplative portraits that are central to his work—emerges a haunting romanticism, all the more unforgettable in the context of the cool, authoritative temperament that was their author. In a picture such as the portrait of "Miss Van Buren" (Fig. 76), the thoroughness of visual and formal analysis and consequent thoughtfulness of composing and rendering is made both human and a work of art through a tender poetry which might make the spectator think of Vermeer.

The saga of the American portrait, from the seventeenth century to Eakins, is not one of the great stories in the history of

Fig. 76—Thomas Eakins: *Miss Van Buren. Ca.* 1889–91. The Phillips Collection, Washington, D.C.

art, for there were too many inferior painters along with such masters as Copley, Ralph Earl, Gilbert Stuart, Whistler, and Eakins. But it is a major story in the history of civilization. It bears continuing analogies with the history of ancient Roman portrait sculpture, and perhaps we could say of both of them that, as concrete manifestations of history and social psychology, rather than as aesthetic finality, they are extraordinary achievements.

The American portrait in the twentieth century has been turned over to photography. This is not because photography can do it better (no Karsh is equal to an Eakins), but because painting, in accord with its own inner logic and direction, turned first to the world of external nature (landscape) and then to a world more inward in experience, more abstract in form, more spontaneous in expression.

Many of these developments were already presaged in the work of Eakins' contemporary, *Albert P. Ryder* (1847–1917), the most advanced American painter of his time. During a long and devoted career Ryder painted a relatively small and uncertain number of canvases and panels. He even painted on leather in an ill-advised technique and with inferior materials, so that much of their effect and a large element of their color is gone. Since Ryder considered himself, and was apparently considered by his contemporaries, to be primarily a colorist, these losses are incalculable. We can guess at what had been when we see an occasional picture that shows traces of this rich, brilliant, and unusual coloring, and we can occasionally find the vanished form in an old photograph. Even as they survive, this small body of pictures is a contender for the highest echelon of American art.

Ryder is unusual among painters in that his reputation with critics * is unequal and rather modest, whereas he is frequently and hugely admired by painters. Surely, a small picture of his, apparently buried in a room filled with larger pictures by other Americans, will slowly expand and gain in power and grandeur until it emerges authoritative and monumental, dominating the rest—even as Ryder's personality, in its own quiet and deep way, dominates the American tradition.

* There are some critics, like Roger Fry (who discovered Ryder for Europeans), who are striking exceptions to this tendency.

Similarly, while Ryder's pictures at first glance are created out of mystery and romance, longer acquaintance reveals a profound base in direct experience of nature. Whoever knows the sea and shore by moonlight will find Ryder's motifs not only haunting dreams but incisive and even inevitable expressions of the essence of that realm of real experience. His clouds, so inventively abstract and expressive in form and touch, are yet keenly observed. He would indeed spend entire nights walking the Jersey shore, returning to his New York studio to sleep the morning and paint into the night. And on a trip to Europe he was wont to spend the night at the rail, gazing into sea and sky.

But such observation was inseparable from empathy, and as Ryder himself said, "What avails a storm cloud accurate in form and color if the storm is not in it?" This empathy somehow formed a universe of which the major elements were nature itself, its workings, and its medium for man; the anonymous human element, whose central form is the toilers of the sea; and his own self-expression, compounded of Shakespeare and Wagner and the Bible, but re-fused in the image of a powerful and singular temperament.

Ryder was known as a recluse, and he certainly lived a life careless of amenity or order (although he had a strong sense of propriety and always dressed formally when he went uptown). He professed that "the artist needs but a roof, a crust of bread, and his easel, and all the rest God gives him in abundance. He must live to paint and not paint to live. He cannot be a good fellow; he is rarely a wealthy man, and upon the 'potboiler' is inscribed the epitaph of his art." Ryder's words are strangely prophetic of both the future lot and battle cry of the twentieth-century painter in an America only recently (and still often for the wrong reasons) aware of the significance of art at all.

Prophetic too (and sometimes damaging because it resulted in too much reworking) was Ryder's absorption in the painting itself, suggestive of a new kind of identity between artist and work that has been crucial in recent American painting. Of one purchaser he remarked, "I was worried somewhat at first by his wanting to take his picture away before I had finished, but lately he has been very nice about it—only comes around once a year or so."

Fig. 77—ALBERT P. RYDER: *Moonlight. Ca.* 1884. The Smithsonian Institution, National Collection of Arts, Washington, D.C.

Ryder's ultimate stature must depend not only on his power and incisiveness, but also on a highly inventive imagination in pictorial conception, as in the "Moonlight" (Fig. 77). Unfortunately for the public, Ryder's pictures, which must be seen in the original, are not very accessible. There is a fine selection in the too-little known Phillips Gallery in Washington, but the best group of all is housed in a small room in the Smithsonian, buried in vast surroundings of naval costumes and stuffed elephants.

The question of the stature of artists such as Eakins and Ryder is a curious one. Certainly they stand head and shoulders above any American contemporaries, even Whistler or Winslow Homer (who did the finest of American water colors). But how do we compare them with their European contemporaries, the great French masters of the late nineteenth century?

In scope, range, and pictorial complexity Eakins is *not* the equal of Cézanne, nor is Ryder of Van Gogh. But it is unsatisfactory to compare them either with the "little masters," for they are too much for Boudin, Monticelli, or even Jongkind. Eakins might be conceivably in a class with Seurat, * and Ryder might be considered a more important artist than Gauguin (not historically, to be sure, but in the sight of the gods). We are, however, presented with the difficulty that the Americans represent a different *kind* of artist.

In the mid-twentieth century, the difference in kind became realized on a world-scale, when American painting took over the reins from a still vital European tradition. Europe, with its residual preference for artistry and its disinclination to test the very bounds of art itself, fell behind.

The major painting of our day is American, and its style or type is variously referred to as Abstract Expressionism, Action Painting, American-type painting, or even the New York School. The first and last of these are the most significant.

During the first half of the twentieth century, there were many fine American painters, and names such as those of *Maurice Prendergast* (admired by Bonnard), *Charles Demuth* (whom Marcel Duchamp called "an artist worthy of the name"), *Arthur Dove, John Marin,* or *Marsden Hartley* are probably still underrated. Dove, one of the first abstract artists anywhere, developed early in the century at the same time as, but independently of, Kandinsky; and Demuth, Marin, and Hartley learned many a lesson from French Cubism and German Expressionism. Yet there is something limited about the style-world of all these

* As is generally true in a comparison of American and European artists of the nineteenth century, Seurat's art is fuller, more comprehensive, more dimensioned, and more final in itself than Eakins'. Both were of a scientific turn of mind, but Eakins' analytic powers were directed toward the object, the phenomenon of nature, whereas Seurat's were directed toward the painting, the phenomenon of art. Thus, Seurat seems to emerge as the larger artist, though the best work of Eakins is very fine and perhaps still underrated. A more helpful kind of comparison (though not within our province here) is that of the American painters with certain American writers of the century—Eakins with Walt Whitman, for example, or Ryder with Poe and Melville.

artists. Between naïve native impulse and the advanced foreign concept something remained misunderstood.

Eakins and Ryder had been able, through a highly selective sampling of European art, to further implement their own intentions without confusion or debilitation. But when the full impact of modern European art hit this continent (notably with the famous Armory Show in New York in 1913), it was as if the American painter had to be overcome by this extraordinary and world-significant phenomenon before he in turn could overcome it and forge from it implements to further his own proper development.

In a sense modern American art could have developed out of the abstract and expressionist possibilities presented by Ryder and Dove, without the intermediation of the great European schools of the twentieth century. But there are certain essential aspects of Abstract Expressionism that might not have evolved without the experience of Miró, Picasso, Beekmann, and other Europeans, and that in any case were in historical fact clearly indebted to them.

The paintings of Ryder and Dove are small and restrained, and their imagery, whether more or less abstract, always has a specific origin and intent. The paintings of *Jackson Pollock, Clyfford Still, Willem de Kooning, Mark Rothko,* and *Franz Kline* (some of the most authoritative and influential American painters of the past twenty years) are typically large, active, and unspecific in imagery or object reference. Kline's "1960 New Year Wall: Night" (Fig. 78) suggests the new order of art.

In the 1920's and 1930's Matisse, Bonnard, Picasso, and Beckmann sometimes painted very large canvases, but these pictures still retained something of an object-like character—in that the spectator had to stand back to see the complete composition. Abstract Expressionist paintings, on the other hand, draw the spectator into them. The field of the canvas is thus larger than the field of vision of the spectator, who finds himself (for the first time since the Gothic) in a world beyond measurement—one which purposely destroys the fixed module of man and leads toward the experience of an infinity of space.

An infinity of time is elicited through the development of a formal style which eschews specific objects or tangible shapes,

Fig. 78—FRANZ KLINE: *1960 New Year Wall: Night*. 1960. Collection: The Art Institute of Chicago. (Courtesy: Sidney Janis Gallery, New York)

and produces an inner transformation of one form into another, one color or accent into another and still another, until time like space has no stop. Earlier abstract paintings like those of Mondrian were composed of strictly confined forms, lines, and colors, and even the more open and fluid paintings of Kandinsky are filled with elements of closed or finite shapes or colors, or with suggestive traces of the object world. To the contemporary eye these are very beautiful but somewhat quaint.

Compared with earlier painting, the Abstract Expressionist type is unprecedentedly centrifugal in its force, bursting with cosmic energy. To speak of a type is partly misleading. There is no specific type in the sense that the paintings of one practitioner could be confused with those of another, as in certain moments of Impressionism or Cubism. One characteristic of the new American painting is the individual independence of personal style, to a degree that mutual influences, which are many, are very difficult to determine—even by the artists themselves.

While abstract art and Expressionism proper both underlie this development, Surrealism too is instrumental. However, the rule of Surrealism here is not that which involves the devising of symbolic forms out of the subconscious (as in so much European painting), but rather the free release of spontaneous pictorial imagery, generally not identifiable but very rich in suggestive power and range. This also produces a high degree of pictorial inventiveness—a persistent trait in American painting.

Where the world of objects is repudiated, the world of nature takes over. This is a field of ever-increasing dimensions, subtleties, and unexpected aspects; but its forms and forces are so frequently of a naturalistic aura that Ryder's realm of emotive imagination, stimulated in specific landscape, appears a direct ancestor.

The paint handling—though varying enormously from artist to artist—is always direct and immediate in sensation, with much carrying power of the specific motor experience of brush, knife, or whatever instrument is used, as well as of the particular qualities of give, spring, or resistance of the canvas or board that provides the painting ground. Here, too, as in the very scope of the painting, the spectator is involved empathically—which is one justification for the term "action" painting.

If these paintings were nothing but action, however, they would not be art. What makes the best of them a very high order of art is of course the creative genius of their composers. But in the meantime it is possible to consider certain combinations of factors that contribute to the complexity of this kind of painting; the resolution of these factors is part of its struggle and its triumph.

For this is emphatically an art of struggle. In these paintings the whole building up of the pictorial conception takes place on the canvas, as contrasted with the older procedure of building from sketches, studies, and drawings before the finished work was laid in. In a typical Abstract Expressionist painting there are a great many other paintings, studies, formations, and reformations underneath the final painting. This sometimes creates a technical problem of support as well as of future condition, but from the present point of view this is simply a mark of the style.

Abstract Expressionist painting in its most ambitious form works toward resolving a number of vital oppositions or dialectics. Some of these might be considered. For one thing, there is usually a polarity between the finiteness of touch in surface and execution, and the infinitude of space and time which is the realm of experience that provides the conscious or unconscious motivation. Similarly, there is a contrast somehow synthesized between the small, highly subjective, and even solipsistic sensation of the artist, and the vast, objective universe that he interprets. Again, there is a tension between the paint experienced as substance or matter, and its disposition and movement experienced as energy. This in turn is related to the opposition between the sense of continuity of the surface (this kind of picture is sometimes referred to as "all-over painting"), and the elements of spontaneity of touch and the varying use of "accidents" which provide qualities of unexpectedness and verve.

One might say, further, that there is a dialogue between the artist's instinct toward *pictorial* form and his stylistic need to deny *objective* form (the rendering of figures or objects), and similarly between a liberated *creative* imagination and energy and the need to *destroy* all impedimenta to this new expression, the need in effect to destroy all older art—a need of great persistence because of an unprecedented awareness of art's historical significance.

Further, there is in Abstract Expressionism a strong contrast between the primordial funding of emotive inspiration and the highly self-aware and sophisticated approach and technique which defines the modern world and the urbane artist who reveals it. And of key importance is the counterpoint between the spontaneous release of unconscious sensations and psychological experience—the impromptu—and the conscious, deliberate, often agonized reworking, reconstruction, manipulation, re-establishment, and final statement of a pictorial problem which is above all involved in *process*. For such reasons, Abstract Expressionist pictures, more than any previous American painting, should be seen in the original.

It is because our best painters show greater dimension, as well as a more thorough confrontation of problems, that they now hold a position of world leadership. It must be emphasized that this is no longer the painting of colonies or provincial states, nor even of a bold new nation. Rather it is the mark of a world center—and here is much of the importance of New York City. The contemporary international American style represents the keenest pulse of time, the most intense exploration of space, and is overall the most receptive to ideas and talents from all parts of the globe. At the same time it forms historically a late and vital stage in the evolution of the painting of the West.

INDEX